SAP BW Ultimate Interview Questions, Answers, and Explanations

By

Anurag Barua

Please visit our website at www.sapcookbook.com

© 2005 Equity Press all rights reserved.

ISBN 0-9753052-8-X

SAP BW Ultimate Interview Questions, Answers, and Explanations 1

Hello reader,

Thank you for buying this book. It is not merely a Q&A book and the questions are not just 'How do you do this?' or 'What is the transaction code for doing that?' Having been on both sides of the interviewer-interviewee divide, I can attest to the sense of frustration you feel when such an interview ends up being an exercise in memorizing. As an interviewer, there is no guarantee that you have found the 'right fit' and as interviewee, you do not want to start working on a project without a strong grasp of the fundamentals.

The questions in this book are therefore intended to test your conceptual understanding of the BW. You will also find several questions that test your hands-on proficiency. The answers will provide you with a good overall understanding of the technology. Regardless of your level of proficiency, you will find reading this book a worthwhile experience. Having said that, I would like to stress that this book is by no means a comprehensive guide to SAP BW. It is not a substitute for training and/or experience but will certainly serve as a handy reference.

A large percentage of the questions in this book are based on features in the latest SAP BW releases (including BW 3.5). Indeed, all the screenshots are based on a BW 3.5 system. However, the concepts generally hold true for the earlier versions also and whenver there are significant departures from earlier versions, I have made every attempt to point out the differences.

The book is split into five sections and each section covers one or more areas in BW.

Introduction

This book is divided into five parts. It contains questions on:

(1) Extraction

(2) Modeling and Configuration

(3) Transformations and Administration

(4) Presentation and Analysis

(5) Performance and Miscellaneous

Each interview question has a question and an answer – that is pretty straightforward – but when you see the guru icon – this is information that represents the highest degree of knowledge in a particular area. So if you're looking for a guru, be sure to listen for an answer sim ilar to those given under the guru icon.

 Don't be bamboozled!

The BW Guru has Spoken!

Anurag Barua

Part I: Extraction

Question 1: Enhance Datasource

How do you enhance a Datasource?

A: Firstly, you need to create an append structure to the extract structure of a DataSource. You can do this by running transaction RSA6 or by running transaction SBIW and then executing the following configuration steps: Postprocessing of DataSources → Edit DataSources and Application Component Hierarchy. This will take you to the screen with all the application nodes. You will have to expand each node until you get to the DataSource that needs to be enhanced. Place your cursor on this DataSource and click on the 'Enhance Extraction Structure' button and create the append structure. Add the desired fields – save and activate the append structure. In order to populate the new fields, you need to add logic to SAP enhancement/customer exit RSAP0001 (in transaction SMOD). This exit/enhancement has 4 (function module) components: 1) EXIT_SAPLRSAP_001 for transaction DataSources, 2) EXIT_SAPLRSAP_002 for (master data) attribute DataSources, 3) EXIT_SAPLRSAP_003 for (master data) text DataSources and 4) EXIT_SAPLRSAP_004 for hierarchy DataSources. You will put your logic/code into an 'include'. Since this single enhancement/exit is used for all DataSources, you will first need to check for the DataSource in your code (by using a 'CASE' – 'WHEN' or 'IF' conditionality).

For any source system running Web AS 6.20 or higher, you can enhance Business Add-In (BadI) RSU5_SAPI_BADI (in transaction SE19). You will have to create your own implementation and enhance method DATA_TRANSFORM (for all non-hierarchy DataSources) and HIER_TRANSFORM (for all hierarchy DataSources).

Question 2: Data Extraction Modes

What are the 2 major modes of data extraction from an SAP source system?

A: This is a little tricky to answer – most candidates seem to treat this as a question on the 2 major update modes: full and delta. With a little prodding, you can coax a good candidate into talking about the 'push' and 'pull' modes. In the 'push' mode, data are posted to intermediate tables or a delta queue by the application in the OLTP system without any initiation on the part of the BW system. The LO, FI-GL, FI-AP extractors use the 'push' concept. In the 'pull' mode, the BW system triggers the extraction from the OLTP system. For delta-enabled 'pull' mode extractors, a delta queue or a timestamp (or any monotonously increasing numeric value) approach provides the deltas. All generic extractors that do full loads use the pull mode. It is important to keep in mind that push or pull, the extraction job takes place only when an InfoPackage is run from the BW system.

Question 3: LO Cockpit

What is the Logistics (LO) Extraction Cockpit? How do you set up the LO Cockpit for extraction?

A: It provides you with one common entry point to enhance, schedule, extract and transfer logistics data from your SAP OLTP system to your SAP BW system. It was first introduced with Plug-In (PI) 2000.1 and was meant to supercede the old approach that was based on LIS (Logistics Information System). The cockpit displays various extract structures grouped by application area (02: Purchasing; 03: Inventory Controling; 11: SD Sales; 13: SD Billing etc.) The transaction code to access the cockpit is LBWE or via customizing/IMG menu by first running transaction SBIW and then Settings for Application Specific DataSources → Logistics → Managing Extract Structures → Logistics Extraction Structure Customizing Cockpit. It holds some advantages over the traditional LIS method.

The following are the steps that must be executed in order to extract LO data using the cockpit:

1) Activate the relevant DataSource. If it's purchasing header data that you want to extract, the DataSource would be 2LIS_02_HDR and if you are

interested in line item information, it would be 2LIS_02_ITM.

2) Replicate the DataSource in BW.

3) Hook up the DataSource to the corresponding InfoSource in the BW system

4) Maintain the extract extructure (by clicking on the pencil icon on the cockpit screen for the relevant extract structure).

5) Activate the extract structure

6) Delete the contents of the setup tables by running transaction LBWG

7) Run the setup job for the relevant extractor

8) Schedule a delta initialization load from the BW system

9) Select the desired update method (preferably 'V3') for your DataSource

10) Start executing the delta loads

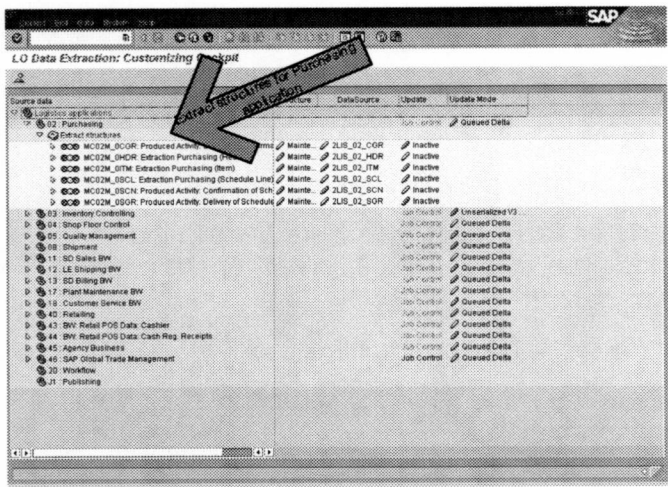

Figure 1: Logistics Extraction Cockpit

Question 4: LO Delta Updates

Starting Plug-In (PI) 2003.1, the LO Customizing Cockpit allows you to assign to an LO DataSource one of three possible methods of delta updates. What are these and explain each.

A: Starting with this PI, SAP the serialized V3 update method has been excluded. So now, there are the following 3 to choose from:

1) **Direct Delta** – Each document posting updates the delta queue without any need for scheduling updates to the delta queue.

2) **Queued Delta** – Instead of the data being written directly to the delta queue for each document change, all changes are temporarily held in an extraction queue. These are then transferred to the delta queue by scheduling a collective update job using reports provided for each application number.

3) **Unserialized V3 update** – This is the latest technique introduced by SAP and for sometime both the serialized and the unserizalized versions were offered concurrently. Starting with PI 2003.1, V3 comes only in unserialized flavor. This method should be used only if you do not care about data serialization. Using a V3 update module, the delta continues to be written to the update tables. They reside there temporarily. A collective update job is scheduled to transfer the data into the delta queue in an unserialized fashion.

Question 5: InfoPackage Groups

What are InfoPackage groups and how do you create them?

A: They are groups of InfoPackages. Usually, extraction jobs that have some kind of kinship are grouped together. The individual InfoPackages can be scheduled as one group for a certain time or they can be scheduled to be executed in a sequence that you specify.

In order to create and execute an InfoPackage group, you need to follow out the following steps on the screen shown in **Figure 2.**

1) In the Administrator Workbench (transaction RSA1), click on the InfoSources tab.

2) On the toolbar of the InfoSources screen, click on the icon for InfoPackage groups (the right-most icon) in order to display another subscreen for InfoPackage groups.

3) Position your cursor on the desired node and right-mouse click and select 'create'.

4) Give your InfoPackage group a name and it is created under the selected node.

5) Drag the InfoPackage from the screen on the left and drop it onto the desired group. Repeat this exercise for all the InfoPackages that you want to put together.

6) Right-mouse click on the InfoPackage group node and select 'Schedule' to schedule the execution of the group or individual packages in the order in which you want them to be executed.

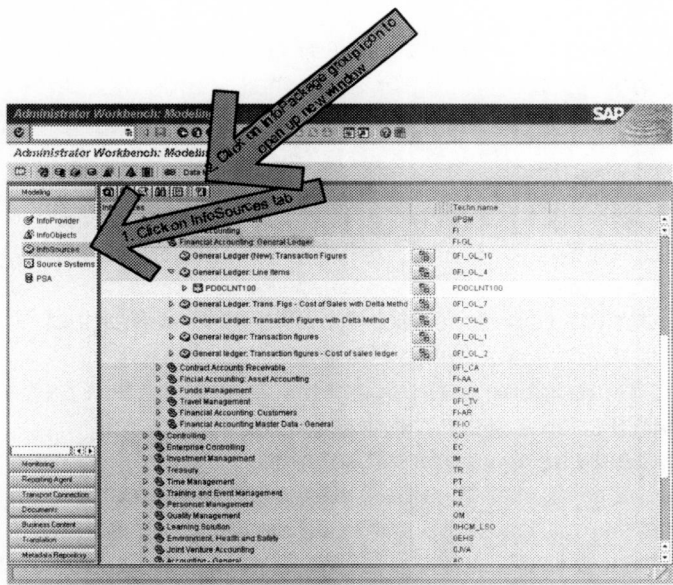

Figure 2: Creation of InfoPackage Groups in RSA1

Question 6: Flat File Extraction

What preparations do you need to make in a BW system in order to extract data from a flat file for the first time?

A: You would create a source system for files in the same way as you would for any other source system. Here are the steps involved:

1) Click on the 'Source System' tab after executing transaction RSA1.
2) On the right-hand panel, position your cursor on 'Source Systems' and from the context menu, click on 'create'.
3) From the pop-up, select the "File System (Manual MetaData, Data Using File Interface" option.
4) In the resulting pop-up, enter a logical system name and a source system name for the file source system and save this information.

If you have several files that you want to extract separately from, you do not need separate file source systems – one will suffice. This is because the actual location of the file is entered in an InfoPackage.

Question 7: Delta Loading

Is delta loading supported for flat files and if so, what are the different options that are available?

A: Delta loading is supported for flat files. Unlike for other DataSources, the options for flat files are rather limited and only two clear options are available:

1) **New status for modified records** – In this option that can be used for loading to ODS Objects only, each record contains the new status for all characteristics and new value for all key figures. It is thus the 'after image' of a record that is sent.

2) **Additive delta** – In this option that can be used for loading data to both ODS Objects and InfoCubes, the target expects the modifications from the DataSource since the previous load. This may happen in one of the following two ways: a) a single record with the difference and b) two records, one containing the reverse image and the other with the after image. As an example, if a key figure has changed from 40 to 10, in the case of (a), the flat file should send a record with −30 as the value for that key figure. In the case of (b), it should send one record with −40 as the value for that key figure (reverse image) and another record with a value of 10 for that key figure (after image). Since the flat file interface does not have the 0RECORDMODE field, the switching of signs has to be manually taken care of in the source file.

There is a 3rd method which even though it shows up as 'Full Upload' can be manipulated to deliver deltas. In this approach a.k.a the psuedo-delta approach, you can set a filter on an InfoPackage that gets changed dynamically by a time-based variable such as a calendar day or month or year. Also, if data for the same time-period exists, it is deleted and the new package is loaded fully. This ensures that even though you are doing a full upload, in reality, you are loading data for those time slices that contain new data or data that have changed since the time they were first loaded into the target.

Question 8: Data Transfer Mechanisms

As of BW 3.5, what are the various data transfer mechanisms that you can use to transfer data into a BW system?

A: As of BW 3.5, there are 6 distinct ways you can transfer data from a source system to a target BW system:

1) **Service API or the SAPI mechanism** – This enables extraction of data from any SAP source system. It comes bundled in the plug-ins that need to be installed on the source system.

2) **Flat file interface** – This simple interface enables extraction of data from flat files that exist in either CSV or ASCII format and reside on either a workstation or application server (preferred method).

3) **DBConnect** – This method allows you to extract data directly from database tables of supported databases.

4) **Business Application Programming Interface (BAPIs)** – This is generally used by 3rd party vendors.

5) **UDConnect or Universal Data Connect** – Available starting release 3.5, this very flexible method enables extraction from virtually all kinds of

source systems. It uses J2EE technology (Java Connector Architecture or JCA) based Java connectors that is part of the Netweaver/Web AS stack, to connect and convert data from all sources into flat files.

6) **XML-based HTTP/SOAP interface** – Data is extracted in an XML format and the corresponding DataSource is created as an XML-based one. Further, there are 3 ways of extracting data that conform to the requirements of this interface – web services, using SAP Exchange Infrastructure (XI) and the Simple Object Access Protocol (SOAP) service.

Question 9: Delta Queue

What is the delta queue in an SAP source system and how does it interact with the target BW system?

A: The BW delta queue is an area where data records are written to for delta updates. This can happen when the underlying application updates the queue during transaction processing ('push' method) or when data is requested by the BW ('pull' method) and thus extracted using a function module and read from the delta queue. Data resides in a compressed form here. This is what happens when you are 'pulling' data: upon initiating a delta initialization in BW (via your InfoPackage), the corresponding DataSource (provided it is delta-enabled) signals to the delta queue that henceforth delta is going to accumulate in the queue.

Let's say that a 1000 new records were added in a week since the delta initialization took place. Now, when you run your delta update, it goes directly to the delta queue and extracts these 1000 records. Upon acceptance of this data in BW, the source system is notified and these records are marked as extracted. Note that these records are not deleted (yet). The following week, 2000 records are created and populated in the delta queue. At this time the queue has 3000 records. When you execute your delta update for the

2nd week, the initial 1000 from the first week are deleted and the 2000 for the 2nd week are extracted and this process continues.

When an application 'pushes' data into a delta queue, the data is more transient in nature and resides there for only the extraction time window.

The delta queue monitor is accessible vis transaction RSA7. A green light for a specific DataSource means that the delta queue is activated for that DataSource.

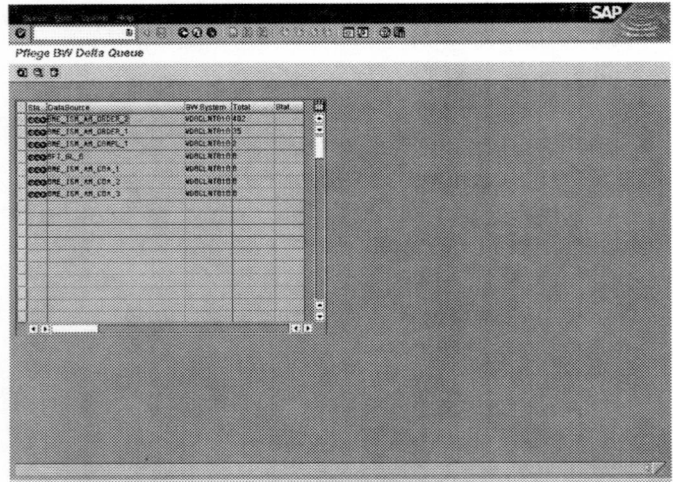

Figure 3: Delta queue in R/3 (transaction RSA7)

Question 10: Explain the purpose of transactions RSA3, RSA5, and RSA6 in an SAP source system.

A:

1) Transaction RSA3 allows you to test extractors and their extracted data in the source system. The tool that is invoked is called the extractor checker. By entering the name of the DataSource, control parameters (such as number of calls to the database, number of records fetched per call etc.) and the selection criteria (based on the input-ready parameters of the extract structure), you can test both the quantity and quality of the extracted data. You can detect errors in extractor logic as well as analyze performance.

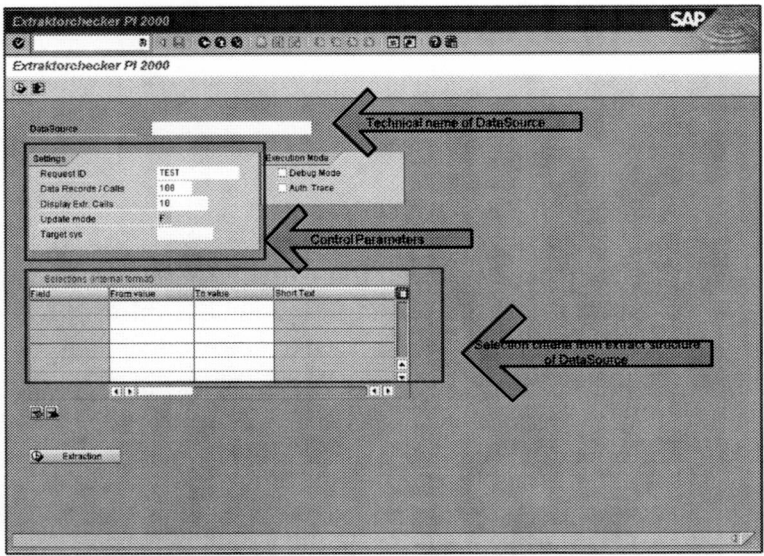

Figure 4: Extractor Checker in Transaction RSA3

2) Transaction RSA5 enables you to install DataSources that are part of standard SAP Business Content. You can use only those DataSources that have been installed. The transaction presents DataSources in the form of hierarchies with the application sitting as one of the highest nodes.

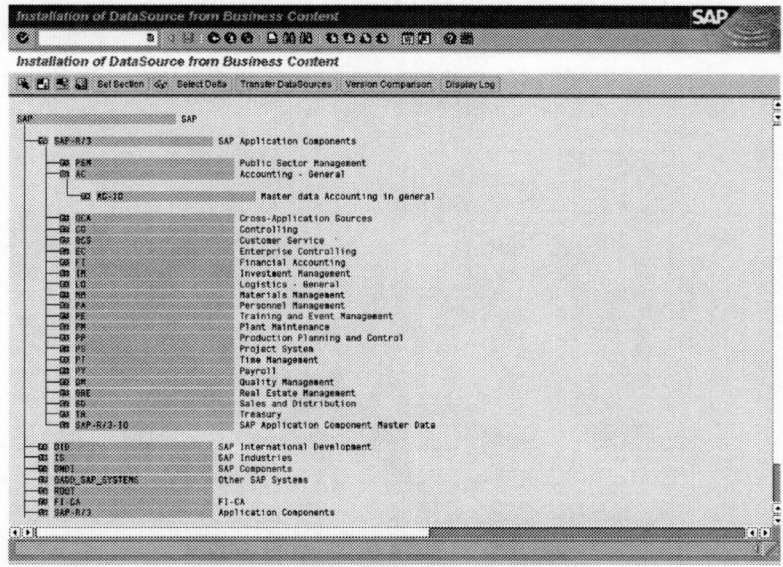

Figure 5 : Installing Business Content in Transaction RSA5

3) Transaction RSA6 allows you to modify the installed Business Content (DataSources). It is also called 'Post process DataSources and Hierarchy'. The information is presented in the form of a hierarchy of nodes (as in transaction RSA5), with the applications sitting as the highest level of nodes and the DataSources inside these nodes. In order to enhance the DataSource you would place your cursor on the relevant DataSource and then press on the 'Enhance Extraction Structure' pushbutton in order to modify the extraction structure of that DataSource. Once you are finished with that activity, you need to click on 'Function Enhancement' in order to populate the fields you have added. You will have the opportunity to add the relevant code in a user exit.

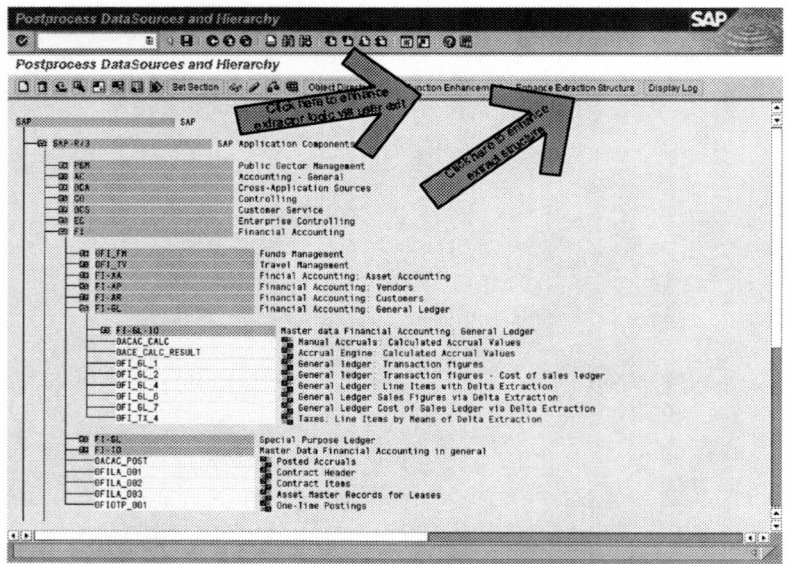

Figure 6: Modifying DataSources in Transaction RSA6

Part II: Modeling & Configuration

Question 11: InfoObject Characteristics

You create a (characteristic) InfoObject 'WIDGETS' in your development system and specify in the maintenance that it has time-dependent master data attributes, texts, is a navigational attribute, and has time-dependent hierarchies. What tables are created when you activate this InfoObject and what is the purpose of each table?

A: A maximum of 11 tables are created:

a) /BIC/SWIDGETS – SID table containing the Surrogate Ids

b) /BIC/TWIDGETS – Table for texts

c) /BIC/PWIDGETS – Time-independent master data attributes of the characteristic 'WIDGETS'.

d) /BIC/QWIDGETS – Time-dependent master data attributes of the characteristic 'WIDGETS'.

e) /BIC/MWIDGETS – Union of PWIDGETS and QWIDGETS or time-dependent and time-independent master data attributes.

f) /BIC/XWIDGETS – Contains SIDs for for time-independent navigational attributes

g) /BIC/YWIDGETS - Contains SIDs for for time-dependent navigational attributes

h) /BIC/HWIDGETS – Table containing all hierarchies of 'WIDGETS'.

i) /BIC/KWIDGETS - Table containing SIDs for all hierarchies of 'WIDGETS'.

i) /BIC/IWIDGETS – Table containing the hierarchy SID structure.

j) /BIC/JWIDGETS – Table containing hierarchy intervals.

Question 12: ODS Object Tables

What are the tables that constitute an ODS object and what happens when you load data from a DataSource into an ODS object?

A: An ODS contains 3 visible tables:

1) **Activation queue table** (if you are on BW 3.0B and above) or **new data table** (if you are on BW 2.1C or below). The activation queue table has the same structure as another ODS table, the change log table. If you are on BW 2.1C or lower, your new data table has the same structure as another ODS table, the active data table.

2) **Change log table.** It's main purpose is to maintain a log of changes (or deltas) in order to update the subsequent data target based on these deltas

3) **Active data table.** It stores data that has been activated in the ODS object.

When you load data into an ODS object, it first gets loaded into the activation queue/new data table. This is where data resides prior to activation and you see the contents of this table when you click on the 'new data' pushbutton in the ODS contents. Upon activation, the active data and change log tables are filled. The new data table is emptied out. At this stage, data in the ODS are ready for reporting (directly off the active data table) and ready to be moved to the next data target (from the change log table).

Question 13: InfoCube Cardinality

When do you check on the 'line item' and 'High Cardinality' flags on a dimension of an InfoCube?

A: A dimension is flagged as a 'line item' dimension when a characteristic in an InfoCube has extremely high cardinality and in fact the cardinality of this dimension is the same as that of the fact table. A good example of this is a characteristic like customer number or document number. Once flagged, no dimension table is created for this 'dimension'. Therefore, the fact table does not have the Dim ID for this characteristic as would be the case normally but has the surrogate ID (SID) directly. So when transaction data is loaded into the InfoCube, Dim Ids are not generated. The advantage is that you not only save space by not having a dimension table but also the join is between two tables (fact and SID) instead of three (fact, Dimension and SID). This makes the query run faster. The disadvantage to using this is that once a dimension is flagged as 'line item', you cannot add additional characteristics.

'High cardinality' dimension is one that has several potential occurences. When you flag a dimension as such, the database is adjusted accordingly. A different index type is used than would be used normally. Generally speaking, if the cardinality is expected to exceed one-fifth that of the fact table, it is advisable to check this flag.

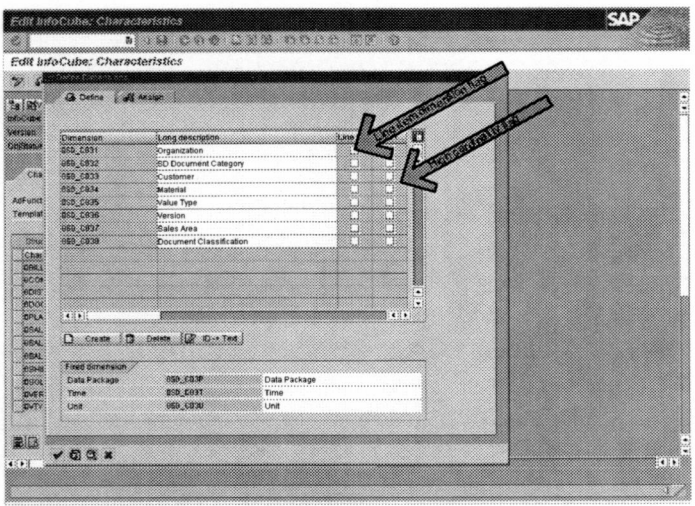

Figure 7 : Line item dimension in InfoCube

Question 14: Delta Loads

Explain the concepts of ROCANCEL and 0RECORDMODE as they relate to delta loads into ODS Objects and their relationship.

A: 0RECORDMODE is an InfoObject in BW that controls the update mode in an ODS Object. ROCANCEL can be considered its counterpart in the source system. If you use a standard extractor delivered by SAP as part of business content, ROCANCEL is filled with an appropriate value and passed onto 0RECORDMODE in the transfer rules of the DataSource. The 'appropriate value' is the update mode for the delta load. The most important ones are ' ' or blank for after image of a record, 'X' for before image, 'R' for reverse image, and 'D' denotes deletion of the record. A standard extractor passes one of these values in a delta load automatically – nothing more needs to be done. However, if a generic extractor capable of delivering deltas needs to be designed, ROCANCEL is not filled automatically and therefore the extractor designer needs to take this into consideration.

An ODS provides three update methods for key figures : Addition, Overwrite, and No update and two for characteristics : Overwrite and No update. Since 0RECORDMODE controls the delta that is used for subsequent loading into data targets, this field is automatically created (in the change log table) when the ODS object is created. 0RECORDMODE is added by default to every DataSource that is delta-enabled. It is another story that it may not get filled automatically.

Depending on whether the update type for a key figure is 'addition' or 'overwrite' in the update rule of an ODS object, delta loads out of it and into a subsequent data target are suitably updated based on a combination of the update type in the update rule (additon or overwrite) and the value in 0RECORDMODE.

Question 15: InfoCube Tables

You are interested in using the sales overview InfoCube 0SD_C03 and would like to know the consitutent tables (and their names) of this InfoCube. How would you do this? What tables make up an InfoCube?

A: Run transaction LISTSCHEMA, in the resulting screen, select the InfoCube type from the dropdown ('B' in this case since it is a BasicCube) and select or type in the InfoCube name ('0SD_C03' in this case). Upon execution, the primary (Fact) table is displayed as an unexpanded node. Upon expansion, you see the following screen:

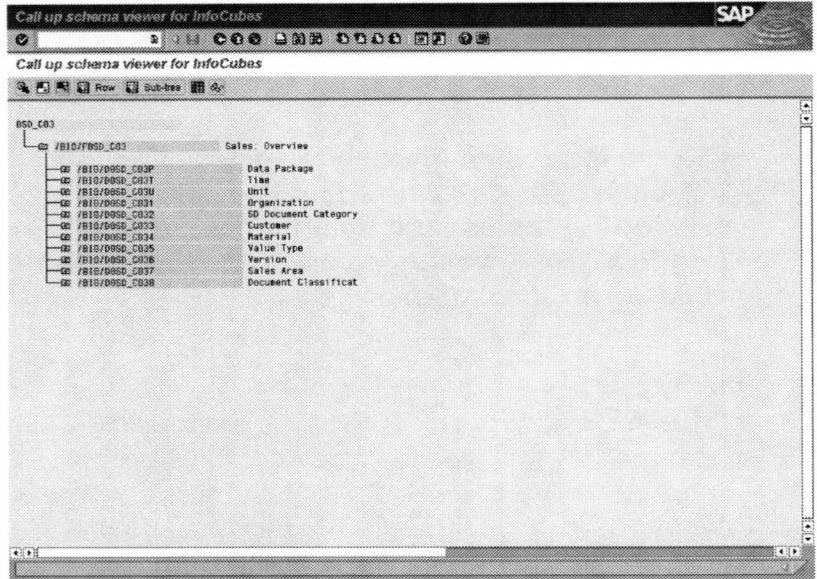

Figure 8: Results from running transaction LISTSCHEMA for InfoCube 0SD_C03

An InfoCube is made up of a fact table and dimension tables. Each InfoCube can have a maximum of 13 user-defined dimensions and has 3 default dimensions for time, package and unit. For an InfoCube that is part of standard SAP Business content, the tables are named as follows:

- /BIO/F[Infocube Tech. Name]   - Uncompressed fact table

- /BIO/E[Infocube Tech. Name]   - Compressed fact table

- /BIO/D[Infocube Tech. Name] P   - Package dimension

- /BIO/D[Infocube Tech. Name] T   - Time dimension

- /BIO/D[Infocube Tech. Name] U   - Unit dimension

- /BIO/D[Infocube Tech. Name] ['n] - User-defined dimensions

The parts in parantheses should be replaced with the technical name of the InfoCube and for user-defined dimensions, 'n' represents the dimension number (1 through 13) in the order in which they are created.

Question 16: Navigational Attributes

Why do you declare certain master data attributes as 'navigational attributes'? How can an attribute that is flagged as navigational in InfoObject maintenance be used in an InfoCube?

A: If your master data has attributes that are display-only, your transaction data contains data that are historical or accurate at the time this transaction was entered in the source system. If however one or more master data attribute(s) has/have changed by the time you query on this data, you will get incorrect results. Navigational attributes resolves this problem by providing access to current values for attributes. This is possible because master data (and attributes) can be loaded independently of transactional data. The advantage of this approach is that any InfoCube can use these navigational attributes and get values that are current for the relevant time slice. While transaction data can provide you with the historical information, a navigational attribute can provide you with attribute values that are current.

Let's take an example: the postal/zip code attribute of a customer in InfoObject 0CUSTOMER. By making it navigational (as is the case), you can get the current zip code of the customer if (s)he has moved by the time you query on an InfoCube with 0CUSTOMER flagged as a navigational attribute.

Since values contained in navigational attributes are read from relevant master data tables at query run time, they introduce a level of performance degradation because of the extra join operation. Therefore, caution needs to be exercised before declaring an attribute as navigational in an InfoCube.

You have to flag an attribute as navigational in the 'attributes' tab in InfoObject maintenance. This is a prerequisite for this attribute to show up with the input-ready checkbox for navigation in InfoCube maintenance – provided the InfoObject is an included characteristic. In the 'Nav attributes' tab of an InfoCube maintenance screen, you switch on the check box next to the respective attribute. This makes it a navigational attribute for this InfoCube. Once you turn on this flag, it behaves like any other dimensional characterisitc of an InfoCube even though its values are stored not in the dimension tables but in master data tables.

Question 17: InfoObject Attributes

On the 'General' tab of an InfoObject maintenance screen, there is a checkbox titled 'Attribute Only'. What is it's purpose?

A: By turning on this checkbox, you are marking this InfoObject as an exclusive attribute. It cannot be used as a navigational attribute but only as a display attribute for another characteristic. Since it cannot serve as a navigational attribute, you cannot include it in an InfoCube. You can however continue to use this attribute in ODS Objects and Infosets. In fact, it can even be flagged as an InfoProvider.

Question 18: InfoCube Modeling

Suppose you are modeling an InfoCube and you need a key figure that holds the number of customers. You create this key figure accepting the SAP defaults like the 'SUM' option for aggregation and 'Summation' for Exception Aggregation. You include this key figure in your cube and run a query (for finding out the number of customers that different goods are sold to) but find that the number of customers that are shown in the results exceeds the actual number. What's wrong with your key figure model and how can you rectify this?

A: This key figure is aggregating the number of customers so that if you have different goods being sold to the same customer, it is adding each occurrence as though it were a unique customer. This is an example of a key figure that is not a cumulative one nor is it non-cumulative. It can be considered semi-cumulative meaning that it adds up the occurrences of customer(s) but needs to have the customer characteristic InfoObject as the exception aggregation characteristic. This ensures that only unique occurrences are counted instead of everything being summed up as would be the case otherwise. Also, the exception aggregation should be set to one of the two counter options (all values or only non-zero values). You would still need to set the aggregation to 'SUM' because within the parameters of exception aggregation, this key figure needs to sum up its values.

Another way of achieving the same output is by bypassing the creation of such a key figure and instead using a formula variable for the customer characteristic and data functions. However, this is a much more complex and rigid option.

Question 19: Analysis Process Designer

What is the Analysis Process Designer (APD) and explain the processes that are available in the APD.

A: It is a tool that was introduced by SAP in BW 3.5. It will enable you to comprehensively analyze data, detect patterns, perform advanced analysis and transformations and store this data. These patterns and relationships are usually not apparent by simple observation. From a user standpoint, it is a workbench (accessible by running transaction RSANWB) with a GUI that enables creation, execution and monitoring of analysis processes using drag-and-drop technology. The APD can also be looked at as the front-end for SAP's data mining capabilities.

The following are the processes that you need to execute in the order given below:

1) Select your desired source (which is actually a data target) in your BW system. The source could be an InfoProvider, characteristic InfoObject, table, query or flat file.

2) Prepare and scrub the data in step 1. This can be done by using one or more of the following techniques: filter, join, aggregation, transpose into rows, transpose into columns, hide columns and sort.

3) Use various transformation functions to identify patterns and relationships. These transformation functions are classic data mining functions like clustering, regression, ABC classfication, decision tree, scoring and ABAP routines.

4) The results are stored or written to data targets such as characteristic InfoObjects, ODS Objects and OLTP systems.

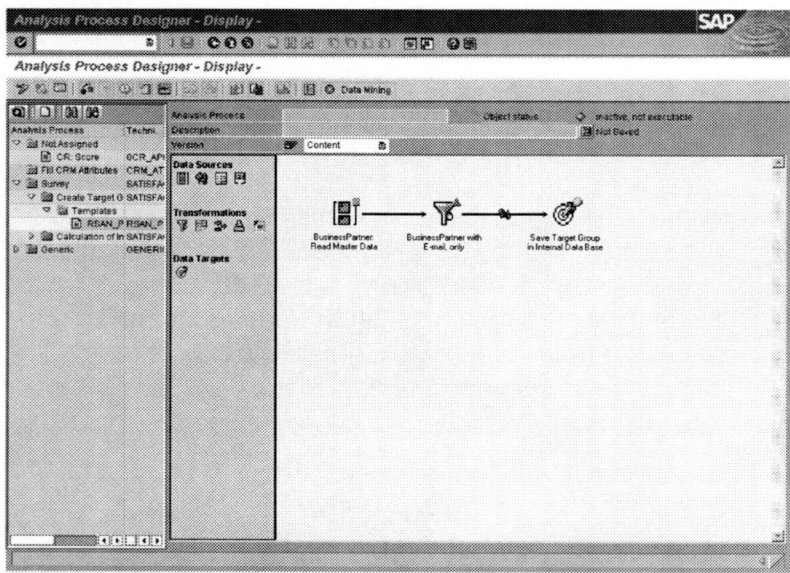

Figure 9: The Analysis Process Designer Workbench (Transation RSANWB)

Question 20: Multiprovider

What are the advantages of using Multiproviders?

A:

1) Generally speaking, when a query is run against a multiprovider, it is split into multiple sub-queries and these run in parallel (unless you actually direct the system to run these sequentially) thereby improving overall query response times.
2) It is not a physical entity and therefore does not occupy any additional space.
3) Even though the constituent InfoProviders may change, it provides a central interface.
4) It enforces better logical partitioning of data. A typical usage of a multiprovider is in combining (a union and not a join as in the case of an InfoSet) data from a plan and an actual InfoCube. Storing plan and actual data in one InfoCube is not optimal and could lead to a sparsely populated InfoCube. By providing the ability to `multiprovide`, the individual cubes can be combined on demand (when a query is executed).

Question 21: ODS Settings

What are the different settings that are available in the maintenance of an ODS? What is the purpose of each setting?

A: There are seven setting options in ODS maintenance. Not all of them can be maintained once you have data in your ODS. Here is a list of the different flags and their explanations:

1) **BEx Reporting** – You need to turn this flag on if you plan on running queries directly on it. In other words, without turning this flag on, an ODS Object will not even show up as an InfoProvider in an InfoArea in BEx. If the flag is not turned on, SIDs are not created for those InfoObjects/characterisitcs that are present in data that are activated. This expedites activation. If an ODS Object is an intermediate data target or is used in an InfoSet, this flag should be kept turned off.

2) **ODS Object Type** – There are two types of ODS Objects: standard and transactional. You can switch only if no data have been loaded into it. Before making the switch though, you need to understand the implications because transactional ODS Objects are used only in special cases.

3) **Unique Data Records** – This indicator's sole purpose is to improve load performance. If you know that only unique records are being loaded, this flag needs to be set. The downside of keeping this flag turned on is that if a record whose key

matches that of an existing record is part of a subsequent load, the process aborts because it assumes that it is a duplicate. You can toggle with this switch after data are loaded.

4) **Check table for InfoObject** – This is really a display-only field and shows you the InfoObject for which this ODS Object is a check table, if that's the case.

5) **Automatically Setting Quality Status to OK** – As the name suggests, when data are loaded into an ODS Object, the quality status (traffic light) automatically turns to green. You do not need to do a manual quality check and change the status. It is advisable to always keep this flag turned on unless you have some strong reason to suspect the quality of the data being loaded.

6) **Automatically Activating the ODS Object Data** – If you set this flag (as indeed you should), activation of loaded data takes place automatically provided that the 'Quality Status OK' (traffic light) is green. Technically it means that data are moved from the new data table to the active data table and the change log table is also updated. However, if the 'Quality Status OK' is not green, the activation does not take place.

7) **Update data targets from ODS Object automatically** – As the name suggests, if you set this flag, a subsequent data target that the ODS Object updates gets automatically updated. There is no need for you to do so manually. A prerequisite for this is that the ODS Object has been successfully activated.

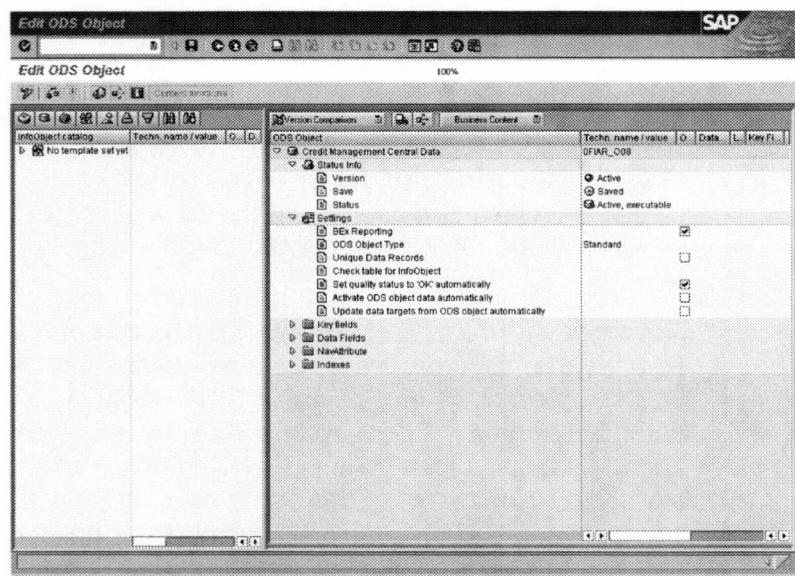

Figure 10: Settings in an ODS Object

Question 22: BEx URL

Your BW system has not been configured for using the Web browser for viewing results of your BEx queries. You would like to know the URL prefix , path and the name of the server. How would you do this?

A: Carry out the following steps:

1) Run function module RSBB_URL_PREFIX_GET in test mode in transaction SE37.

2) There are 3 import parameters, 'I_HANDLERCLASS', 'I_PROTOCOL' and 'I_MESSAGESERVER'. Do not change the default value in the first parameter. Delete the 'X' value from the 'I_MESSAGESERVER'. Execute.

3) You get all your required information in the results screen: the export parameter 'E_URL_PREFIX' contains the URL prefix, 'E_URL_PATH' contains the path, and 'E_URL_SERVER' contains the name of the server.

Question 23: Master Data Special Chars

You are loading master data and it contains some special characteristics and your loads are failing. What would you do to enable your BW system to accept these special characteristics?

A: You need to run transaction RSKC or in the IMG of the BW system, go to SAP Business Information Warehouse → General BW Settings → Maintain permitted extra characters. A screen with a single input field 'Permitted Extra Characters' is displayed. Enter the desired special/extra character and click on the execute icon. The special/extra characters are stored on the database in table RSALLOWEDCHAR.

In BW, a character that is not found in the following set: *-!"%&"()*+,-./:;<=>?_0123456789ABCDEFGHIJKLMNOPQRST UVWXYZ]* is a special/extra character.

A quick and easy way of checking the character set that SAP allows (the default) as well as the user-defined special/extra characters is by running function module RSKC_ALLOWED_CHAR_GET. Output parameter

E_ALLOWED_CHAR displays the completed list of characters (default + user-defined), E_DEFAULT_CHAR displays the default characters and E_USERDEF_CHAR displays the user-defined characteristics.

The number of user-defined characteristics that can be entered is limited to 72. If your data has more than 72 unique user-defined characteristics, you will have to use certain workarounds.

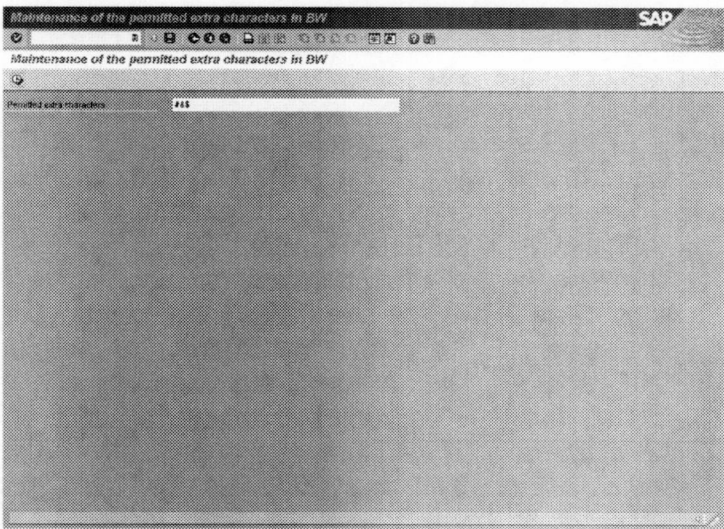

Figure 11: Maintenance of special characters

Question 24: Control Parameters

What are the different control parameters that you can maintain for data transfer from an SAP system; what is the name of the table that stores this data and what customizing option in the IMG allows you to maintain this table?

A: In an SAP system, you can maintain parameters that control the size of the data packages, the frequency of IDocs etc. These values are stored in table ROIDOCPRMS and to maintain these settings in the IMG, you need to run transacation SBIW and then open up node 'General Settings' and then execute 'Maintain Control Parameters for Data Transfer'.

The following are the actual parameters:

1) **Max. Size** – It is the size (in Kb) that meets your requirement for a certain maximum size of your data packages. Keep in mind, this is not the actual size of your data package but has an influence on the actual size. If no parameter is maintained, the SAP default of 10 MB or 10000 KB is used. Also, this setting may be overriden by logic in individual extractors.

2) **Max. Lines** – It is the number of records that are transferred in one data package.

The actual size of a data package is computed using the following formula:

(MAXSIZE * 1000) / width of transfer structure

→ If MAXLINES > the result of the formula, package size is the result of the formula.

→ If MAXLINES < the result of the formula, package size is set to MAXLINES.

If no value is maintained for this parameter, the SAP default of 100,000 records is used.

3) **Frequency** — It controls the frequency with which an Info Idoc is sent after a Data Idoc. It allows for efficient monitoring and management of your data loads. If no value is maintained, the SAP default of 1 is used.

4) **Max. Processes** — This parameter controls the maxium number of parallel dialog work processes that can be used during data extraction provided they are available. What this really means is that you might want to specify a large number of processes thinking that this will ensure maximum parallellism. What is you actually get to use is what is available during extraction. When nothing is specified, the SAP default of 2 is used.

Question 25: BW Object Versions

Name and explain the different versions of BW objects.

A: 5 object versions exist for BW objects. They are:

1) D – All objects delivered by SAP in standard Business Content are in 'D' state, as long as they are not modified.

2) A – This is the active version and for a transport containing an object to be imported into the target system successfully, an object must be in the active state. Business Content objects that are activated will be in this state.

3) M – This is the modified version. An object that is in the 'A' state may move to 'M' state when it is changed.

4) T – This is the temporary or transport version. It is the temporary version in which source system-dependent objects.

5) N – This is another temporary version.

Question 26: Transactional InfoSource

When you create an InfoPackage for a transactional DataSource/InfoSource, what are the four processing options that are available and explain each.

A: The 4 processing options are:

1) **PSA and then into Data Targets (Package by Package)** – When this option is chosen, data are loaded into the PSA package by package (i.e. serially). A work process is created for each package and once the data in the package are successfully loaded onto the PSA tables, the same work process then writes data onto the data target.

2) **PSA and Data Targets in Parallel (Package by Package)** – In this mode, two work processes are created, one for posting data in the PSA tables and the other for posting data into the data target. If the data are successfully posted into the PSA, the 2nd work process for loading data into the data target is spawned provided there is at least one work process available. Both processing of requests and posting of data happens in parallel. The critical requirement for this sort of parallellism to work is the availability of dialog work processes.

3) **Only PSA/Update Subsequently in Data Targets** – If this option is selected but the 'Update Subsequently in Data Targets' checkbox is not flagged, only the PSA is loaded with data. A dialog work process is created for each package and the

PSA is loaded serially, package by package. If the 'Update Subsequently in Data Targets' checkbox is turned on, the subsequent data target is updated automatically in serial fashion, package by package and work process by work process.

4) **Data Targets Only** — This option ensures that the PSA is bypassed and data are loaded directly to the data target. Obviously, this method minimizes the usage of system resources but the trade-off is that you do not get an option for checking data inconsistencies and errors and possibly correcting them. This method is recommended only for flat file loads and generally if there is complete confidence in the completeness and contents of the DataSource.

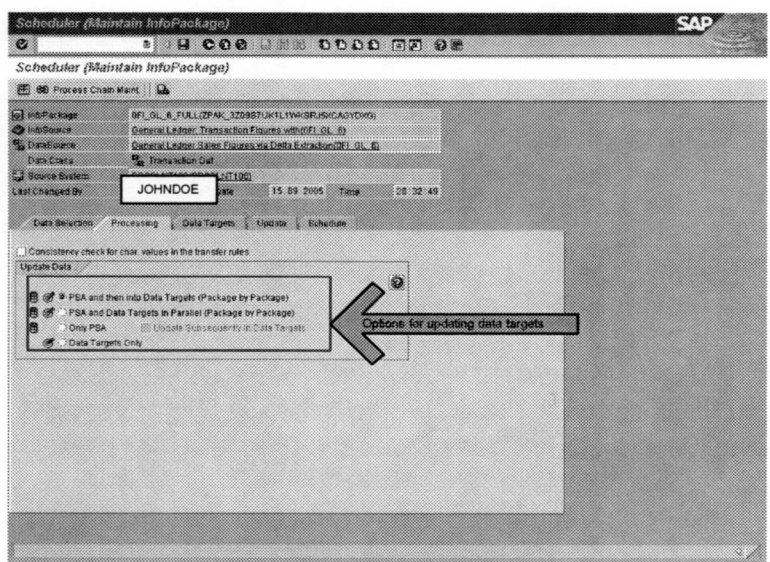

Figure 12: Data target update options in InfoPackage

Question 27: InfoCube Types

What are the different types of InfoCubes? Explain each type .

A: InfoCubes come in two major flavors – Basic InfoCubes or BasicCubes and remote InfoCubes or VirtualCubes:

1) **BasicCubes** – These are physically available in the same BW system in which they are specified or their metadata exist. They can be further sub-divided into:

   a) **Standard InfoCubes** – This is the most common flavor. Most of the standard Business Content InfoCubes are standard ones. Such InfoCubes are optimized for read access, have update rules that enable transformation of source data and loads can be scheduled.

   b) **Transactional InfoCubes** – These are not frequently used and used only by certain applications such as SEM and APO. Data are written directly into such cubes bypassing update rules. While Basic InfoCubes are optimized for read access, transactional InfoCubes are optimized for write access. Based on the database on which these are built, they differ from standard cubes in the way they are indexed and partitioned.

2) **RemoteCubes** – While BasicCubes physically reside on the same database as their metadata, RemoteCubes reside on a remote system. From the

point of view of their definition or metadata in a certain BW system, they can be considered virtual. They come in 3 different flavors:

a) **SAP RemoteCube** – The cube resides in another SAP R/3 system and communication is via the Service API (SAPI)

b) **General RemoteCube** – The cube resides in a non-SAP R/3 source system and is available via the remote InfoCube BAPI.

c) **Remote InfoCube with Services** – The cube resides in any remote system (SAP or non-SAP) and is available via a user-defined function module.

Question 28: Infosource Definition

What is an InfoSource and what flavors does it come in?

A: There are two ways to look at an InfoSource – inside-out and outside-in. In the inside-out view, an InfoSource is a collection of InfoObjects that can be logically grouped. This grouping is the result of the commonality among these objects in terms of a business transaction or business information. These grouped InfoObjects reside in a communiction structure for subsequent updates to data targets connected to the InfoSource.

In the outside-in view, one or more DataSources can be assigned an InfoSource. The individual fields from various DataSources are mapped to corresponding InfoObjects using transfer rules. The transformed data is then subjected to another round of data target-specific transformations via the update rules before they are passed to one or more data targets.

InfoSources come in two flavors:

1) **InfoSources with direct updating** – This method is used for updating InfoObject master data (text, attributes and hierarchies) only. A DataSource delivers (master) data to an InfoObject without applying any update rules but using transfer rules only.

2) **InfoSources with flexible updating** – In this method, data from one or more DataSources is first transformed via transfer rules and then updated

from the communication structure to one or more data targets (master data, ODS Objects, InfoCubes) via update rules for each data target. Starting BW Release 3.0A onwards, both transaction and master data (text and attributes only, not hierarchies) can be updated flexibly. Before this release only transaction data (targets) could be subjected to this mode by an InfoSource. There is thus no difference between transaction and master data InfoSources starting BW Release 3.0A.

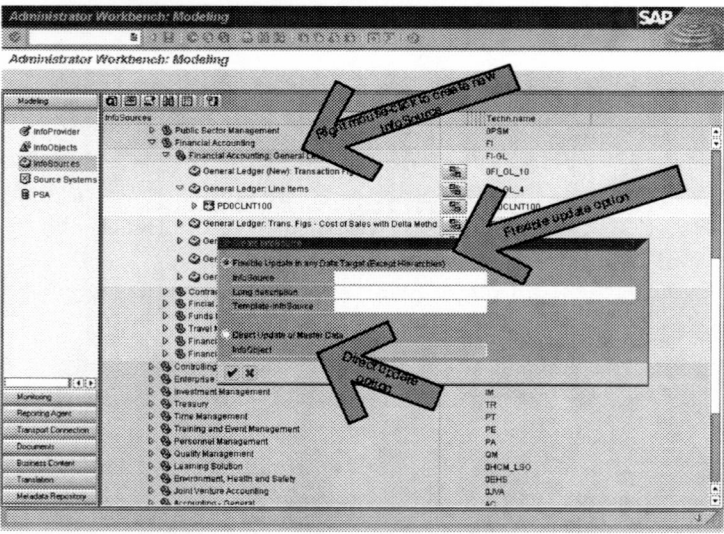

Figure 13: Choosing the correct type of InfoSource

Question 29: Characteristic Hierarchies

How do you create hierarchies for characteristic InfoObject?

A: There are 2 ways to create hierarchies in a BW system:

1) From the SAP menu, carry out the following navigation: Modeling → Master Data Maintenance → Hierarchies. A pop-up ('Initial Screen Hierarchy Maintenance') is displayed. You need to select the InfoObject for which you want to create a hierarchy from the dropdown for 'Restriction on hierarchy basic char'. Upon clicking the create icon, another pop-up is displayed. You have to enter the hierarchy name and description. Once you press enter, you are taken to the actual hierarch maintenance screen.

2) In the modeling area of the administrator workbench (transaction RSA1), click on the InfoObjects to take you to the InfoObjects view. Highlight the desired InfoObject and right mouse-click on it and select the 'create hierarchy' item. It will display a pop-up wherein you have to enter the hierarchy name and description. Once you press enter, you are taken to the actual hierarch maintenance screen.

Question 30: Hierarchy Object Meaning

What does each of the following options in the 'Hierarchy' tab of a characteristic InfoObject maintenance screen mean:

Hierarchy not time-dependent

Entire hierarchy is time-dependent

Time dependent hierarchy structure

A: These are the three time-related dimensions of hierarchy maintenance. They mean the following:

a) **Hierarchy not time-dependent** – This is the default option. When this is set, it means that relationships between nodes and the actual values remain constant over time.

b) **Entire hierarchy is time-dependent** – By choosing this option, you are ensuring that the hierarchy has different versions for different time intervals. The time interval is created when you maintain the properties of the InfoObject. You need to enter 'valid from' and 'valid to' dates.

c) **Time dependent hierarchy structure** – Instead of the entire hierarchy being time-dependent, you can specify which node(s) is/are time-dependent. When you display hierarchies that have time-dependent hierarchy structures, you see nodes or leaves that have different values in different time intervals in different places.

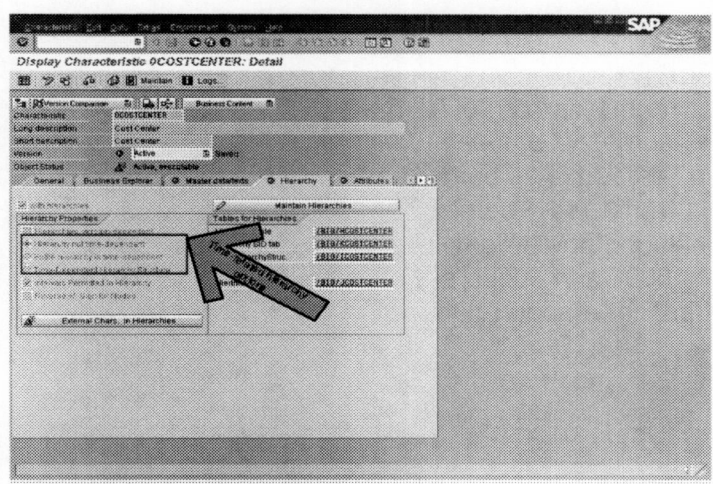

Figure 14: Hierarchy properties in InfoObject maintenance

Part III: Transformations & Administration

Question 31: Splitting Records

How can you split a record coming out of the communication structure of an InfoSource into multiple records?

A: By using return tables. This is one of the options that are available for an update rule for a key figure.

Since this a feature of the update routine, you will have to write your own logic to actually achieve this split. The interface is automatically generated and there are some changes that you will notice: instead of a 'RESULT' parameter in a normal update routine (which would hold a single value), you will now see a 'RESULT_TABLE' parameter. This is a table that will hold all the values the single record has been split into. You will see an additonal 'using' parameter 'ICUBE_VALUES'. Both the 'RESULT_TABLE' and 'ICUBE_VALUES' table reference the same structure and contains the fields of your data target in a denormalized form.

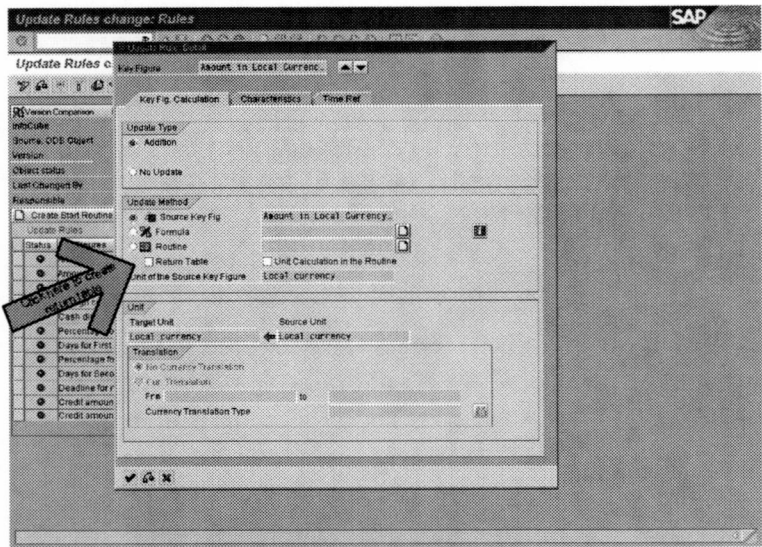

Figure 15: Return table in update rules

Question 32: Transfer Rules

What are transfer rules and what are the different kinds of transfer rules?

A: Transfer rules are a mechanism by which you can apply transformations to your source data at different levels in the BW. They apply both on an individual level (InfoObjects) and a combined level (InfoSource). Transfer rules created on an InfoObject level (in the InfoObect maintenance) are invoked each time the corresponding InfoObject is used in any transfer rule(s). This is generally used to ensure that there is system-wide uniformity in the usage of an InfoObject. Such a transfer rule comes in a single flavor: a transfer routine in ABAP.

Transfer rules created on an InfoSource level represent the transformation from the transfer structure to the communication structure of the InfoSource. They are valid for each unique combination of DataSource and InfoSource and thus do not have any system-wide impacts. Such rules can be created in one of four different ways:

1) **InfoObject** – This is a direct assignment of a field in the DataSource/transfer structure to the corresponding InfoObject in the InfoSource.

2) **Constant** – This is an assignment of a constant value to the InfoObject in the InfoSource. This usually happens when the field in the DataSource/transfer structure does not hold any

value and it becomes necessary to assign a value in the BW.

3) **Routine** – You can add business logic/transformation rules in a routine (using ABAP code). A transformation in a routine is frequently used to realize transformations that are not relatively straightforward.

4) **Formula** – Using the transformation library that contains several different functions (mathematical, logical, date, string etc.) you can assign reasonably complex formulas to an InfoObject in the InfoSource.

Question 33: Open Hub Service

What is the Open Hub Service and what are its components?

A: It is a service (made available with SAP BW 3.0B) that facilitates the distribution of data from an SAP BW system to other applications and external data marts. Objects in the BW system thus become the source of the data – these objects could be InfoObjects or InfoCubes or ODS Objects or a combination of the first three objects resulting in multiproviders. The mapping between the source and the target is made possible by an InfoSpoke which essentially performs the same role as an InfoSource does between a DataSource in the source system and a data target. The targets of an InfoSpoke are flat files, database tables and non-SAP 3rd party application using APIs.

The service has the following components:

1) InfoSpoke – This has 3 components:

    a) Open Hub DataSource which represents the source of the data.

    b) Open Hub Destination which represents the target of the data

    c) Extraction mode which provides both full and delta updates

2) Open Hub Monitor – It allows you to monitor extraction jobs that you trigger when you execute

your InfoSpoke. It is similar to the InfoPackage job monitor.

Keep in mind that the usage of Open Hub Service comes with strings attached. There are license issues that you need to first understand before you make use of this service.

Question 34: Inversion Routine

What is an inversion routine in a transfer rule/routine?

A: An inversion routine is used to pass and transform the selection criteria for a certain navigation in a query to a format that is acceptable to the corresponding selection criteria of the report or transaction in the SAP system. This is the case when you use the Report-to-Report Interface (RRI). It is also used with SAP RemoteCubes since such a cube does not reside in the same system as does its metadata. So, it becomes necessary for the corresponding extractor to receive the selection criteria of the executed query or navigation in the correct format.

An inversion routine is created inside a transfer routine of a transfer rule. In fact, the interface is already made available – the code needs to be filled in by you. Once you select the 'Routine' radio-button and give your routine a name and select one or more of the available fields, you are taken to the routine editor. An inversion routine can be identified by the naming convention – each such routine starts with the word 'INVERT_' followed by the technical name of the InfoObject selected.

Question 35: Start Routine

What is a start routine in an update rule?

A: A start routine in an update rule (to a data target such as an InfoCube or ODS Object) accepts the whole data package, applies transformations to this collection of records and stores these records or the package in a table or structure that is accessible globally. The application of business logic or application of transformations are done in ABAP. All nature of changes are made to the table 'DATA_PACKAGE'. Additionally, user-defined messages can be sent to a monitor using a table 'MONITOR' that is provided in the interface of the start routine.

Some typical transformations that are effected in a start routine are:

- Deletion of certain records based on certain criteria

- Dropping of whole package if required (by setting ABORT = 1) in the start routine code.

- Addition of additional records based on certain criteria.

- If additional transformations/calculations are to be done that require repeated access to certain data (like configuration data), a static variable or a static table in the start routine is the best place to hold this information. This enhances performance.

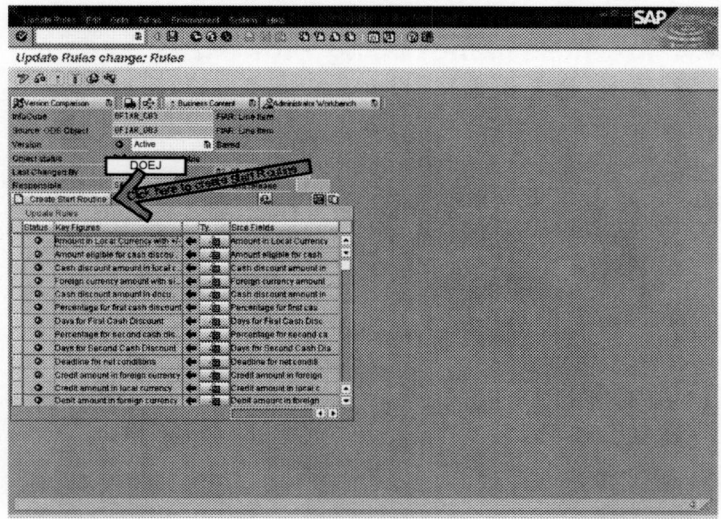

Figure 16: Creating a Start Routine in an Update Rule

Question 36: ROOS Tables

What are the BW-specific tables in an SAP source system whose names being with 'ROOS' and what are they used for?

A: 1) ROOSFIELD – Datasource fields

3) ROOSGEN – Generated Objects for OLTP source

4) ROOSGENDLM – Generic delta management for DataSources

5) ROOSGENDLT – Generic delta management for DataSources (texts)

6) ROOSGENQ – Generic coding for DataSources (only for delta queue at present)

7) ROOSGENQV – Extract structure versions

8) ROOSGENQVF – Field descriptions for extract structure versions

9) ROOSGENRT – Generated object for OLTP source

10) ROOSGENSEG – Generated object for OLTP source but with different time fields then ROOSGENRT.

11) ROOSOURCE – Table header for OLTP sources

12) ROOSOURCET – Texts for an OLTP source based on the sources in ROOSOURCE.

13) ROOSPRMS – Control parameters per DataSource

14) ROOSPRMSC – Control parameters per DataSource channel

15) ROOSPRMSF – Control parameters per DataSource but with some different fields than ROOSPRMS.

16) ROOSSHORTN – DataSource short name

Question 37: Authorization Objects

Name the 2 authorization object classes for BW, describe them and their purpose.

A: Authorization in BW is split into 2 categories – authorization for the workbench and authorization for reporting. Accordingly, authorization object class RS helps you control back-end/administration/workbench activities and RSR is for reporting. Several authorization objects are supplied as part of standard business content by SAP for authorization object class RS. Some examples are S_RS_IOBJ for InfoObject authorization, S_RS_ADMWB for controlling access to objects of the Adminstrator Workbench, S_RS_ICUBE for access to InfoCubes, S_RS_ODSO for access to ODS objects. No authorization objects are supplied with the RSR authorization object class.

Question 38: Security Profile

As a BW administrator, what are the different profiles you need to successfully carry out all tasks in the Administrator Workbench (AWB)?

A: You need certain profiles in both the BW and source systems. In the BW system, you need to have S_RS_ALL and in the source system, you need the following three:

1) B_ALE_ALL: These are authorizations for all ALE/EDI relevant authorization objects.

2) S_IDOC_ALL: These are authorizations for all relevant IDOC activities.

3) S_A.CUSTOMIZ: These are authorizations relevant to all system activities.

Question 39: Authorization Objects

What is the name of the authorization object for BEx query definitions, what is its purpose, what are the fields of this object and what are the possible values for those that have values?

A: It is S_RS_COMP. It enables you to control display, creation, change and deletion of queries. Using values for different fields you can go from one extreme (and make the check very general as in a check for InfoArea or InfoCube) or very specific (a particular restricted key figure in a particular InfoCUbe).

This authorization object has five fields:

1) **Activity (ACTVT)** – The valid activities for this field are create (01), change (02), display (03), and delete (06).

2) **InfoArea (0RSINFOAREA)**

3) **InfoCube (0RSINFOCUBE)**

4) **Component Type (0RSZCOMPTP)** – This field identifies the component and can be the entire query (REP), variable (VAR), calculated key figure (CKF), restricted key figure (RKF), and structure (STR).

5) **Component Name (0RSZCOMPID)** – This is the actual component based on the component type. If you have chosen 'VAR' as the component type, you will need to specify a variable that you want to be checked for authorizations.

Question 40: Process Chains

What is a process chain and what are the advantages of using one? What are the components of every process in the context of a process chain?

A: A process chain enables the scheduling and administration of BW-related tasks and activities. It is a sequence of processes. Starting release 3.0, a centralized user interface (accessible by running transaction RSPC) provides the ability to create, maintain and monitor process chains. It directly supercedes the event chain technology that was used in prior releases and also makes the usage of InfoPackage groups redundant. The advantages of using process chains are manifold – it helps you model and realize complex dependencies in processes and event using drag-and-drop technology and makes it easier to monitor these processes.

There are 4 components of each process:

1) **Process Type** – It is a certain type of process like attribute change run, aggregate rollup, data load etc.

2) **Process Category** – It is the category to which a process belongs. Every process type belongs to one of four categories.

3) **Variant** – Like an ABAP report, each process can have several variants. However, when a process is being executed, only one variant is used.

4) **Instance** – Since process chains used object-oriented technology (and ABAP OO in particular), when a process in run, an instance of the specific process type object is created. It contains run-time information including variant values and messages.

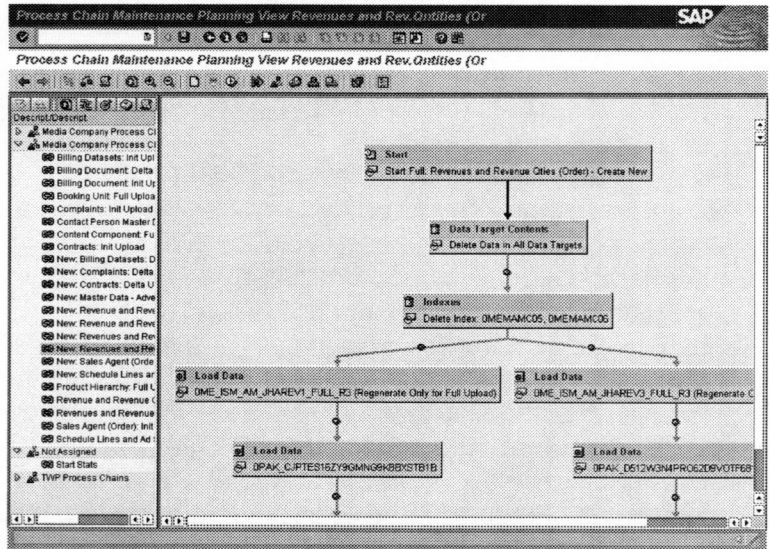

Figure 17: A process chain (in maintenance planning view)

Question 41: Process Categories

What are the 4 process categories delivered by SAP and the process types in each category?

A: They are:

1) **General Services** – This category includes start processes (which is a must for each process chain), boolean processes that help to logically combine different process (AND, OR, and EXOR), ABAP programs, operating system commands, local and remote process chains.

2) **Load Process and Subsequent Processing** – This category contains all processes relevant to loading data into various BW targets. They are data loading process, read PSA and update data target, saving of hierarchies, further processing of ODS Object Data, Data Export into External Systems and Deletion of overlapping requests from InfoCube.

3) **Data Target Administration** – This category contains all process types that are available for administration of data targets. These are deletion of indexes, generation of indexes, constructing database statistics, initial filling of new aggregates, compression of InfoCubes, activation of ODS Objects and deletion of contents in data targets.

4) **Other BW Processes** – This is the miscellaneous category containing process types of attribute change runs, adjustment of time-dependent aggregates, and deletion of requests from the PSA.

Question 42: RSCRM_BAPI

What is RSCRM_BAPI?

A: It is a transaction (code) that has been available since BW 2.1C. It enables you to extract query results from your BW system and dump them into a table or a file or return them to the calling transaction. Prior to generating these results, MDX statements are generated from the query results and these are then transferred to the ODBO interface. A lot of the functionality provided by this RSCRM_BAPI has now been incorporated into the Open Hub.

This transaction has some notable limitations. It does not support queries that use certain logical and mathematical operators, filter and variable values that contains special and lower_case characters etc. Another restriction is when query results are dumped onto a table, the combined length of the key fields cannot exceed 255 characters.

Caution is to be exercised when using this transaction because there could be licensing issues whenever you export data out of SAP BW (and thereby use the BW as an Enterprise Data Warehouse).

Question 43: Reporting Agent Features

What are the various features of the Reporting Agent and how do you access the workbench?

A: It is a workbench that allows you to schedule various reporting functions offline. The RA has the following features:

1) Running of exceptions in background and notification of results. The latter takes different forms namely the sending of alerts via the alert monitor, notification via e-mail and export via BAdI RSRA_ALERT_BADI.

2) Queries can be scheduled for background/offline printing. The query results can be configured to be sent directly to a printer, as an e-mail and spool.

3) Precalculation of web templates

4) Allows the filling of precalculated value set variables in the background.

5) It allows users to display and delete bookmarks. The ability schedule deletion of bookmarks (in the background) is valuable because there is no other automated mechanism to do this.

6) Allows you to precalculate queries in the background for Crystal Reports. Since this technique is similar to caching or prequerying, it improves performance.

The RA workbench is available via a tab (the 3rd one) in the BW administration workbench (transaction RSA1) or by directly running transaction RSREP. The screen looks like this (as shown below):

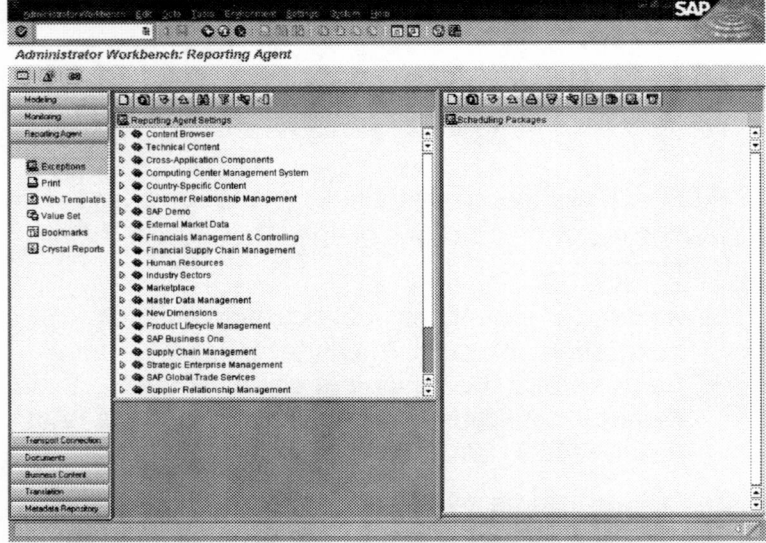

Figure 18: Reporting Agent Workbench

Question 44: Reporting Agent Realization

What are the 3 general steps you need to take to realize most of the features of the Reporting Agent.

A: Except for the maintaining of bookmarks, the other 5 functions (as detailed in the answer to Question 43) can be realized by executing the following 3 steps in order:

1) For each function, make the relevant settings.

2) Assign each unique combination of settings to a scheduling package.

3) Schedule the scheduling package as a background job or in a process chain. Keep in mind that you can use process chains only from BW 3.X onwards.

Part IV: Presentation & Analysis

Question 45: Virtual Key Figures

What are virtual key figures and virtual characteristics? Why and how do you use them?

A: Virtual key figures and characteristics are InfoObjects in InfoCubes or master data attribute tables that do not store values in the database. They are created as normal InfoObjects and the virtual characteristics are assigned to dimensions in InfoCubes just like other characteristics. However, they are unassigned meaning the update rules do not assign any values to them.

Sometimes values for certain characteristics and key figures can be derived (or makes sense to be derived) only dynamically. An example of this could be the calculation of a key figure whose value is based on a dynamically changing master data attribute. Or it is possible that such a calculation may be complex enough for the functions in the BEx Query Designer not to be able to satisfy. You would use virtual key figures and characteristics in such situations. They are populated dynamically during query execution.

You have to declare your virtual object and program your logic for these dynamic calculations in user exit **EXIT_SAPMRSRU_001** i.e. enhancement **RSR00001.** The declaration is done in program

ZXRSRTOP and the calculation logic is done in program **ZXRSRU02.**

Virtual key figures and characterisics should be used with caution because of several disadvantages in using them. They have an adverse impact on query performance because they are computed dynamically when a query is executed. They cannot be used in conjunction with aggregates – a major shortcoming. You cannot use caching because using caching would mean that data will not be gotten from the InfoCube each time a query is executed but will be reused from the cache. This means that the user exit **EXIT_SAPMRSRU_001** will not be invoked each time and this would mean that the virtual key figures and characteristics are not populated.

Question 46: Variable Processing Types

What are the different processing types for a variable?

A:

1) **Default value/user entry** – This type allows use to define a default value for a variable during the creation of a query. If the variable is not ready for input, then the default value is used as the value of the variable. If it is ready for input, the default value is shown in the input field of the variable but a user can enter a value and override the default.

2) **Replacement Path** – A replacement path (eg:- the results of one query) is specified as the value of the variable. The value gets populated upon query execution.

3) **Customer Exit** – Enhancement RSR00001 is used to code the logic needed to populate the variable during query execution.

4) **SAP Exit** – These are delivered with Business Content and while a customer can use them (automatically, when you use the SAP-delivered variable), you (customer) cannot assign a processing type of SAP Exit to a variable.

5) **Authorization** – When a query is executed, the relevant data are selected as per the user's authorizations.

Question 47: Query Read Modes

What are the three different read modes of a query?

A: They are:

1) **Read all data** – When a query is run, all data are read from the database. Obviously, queries run in this mode place a heavy burden on system resources. It should be used when all the data is indeed needed especially for trend analysis or data mining

2) **Read data during navigation** – Choosing this option ensures that only data that are strictly required are returned. Data are fetched on demand during navigation. Obviously, this option ensures that system resources are used judiciously.

3) **Read data during navigation and expanding hierarchies** – Choosing this option means that not only are data fetched on demand but in the case of characteristics with hierarchies, data for only those hierarchy nodes that are expanded are retrieved.

The desired mode can be set in transaction RSRT. On the first screen, click on the 'properties' push-button and in the 'Query properties' pop-up, select the desired mode from the 'read mode' drop-down.

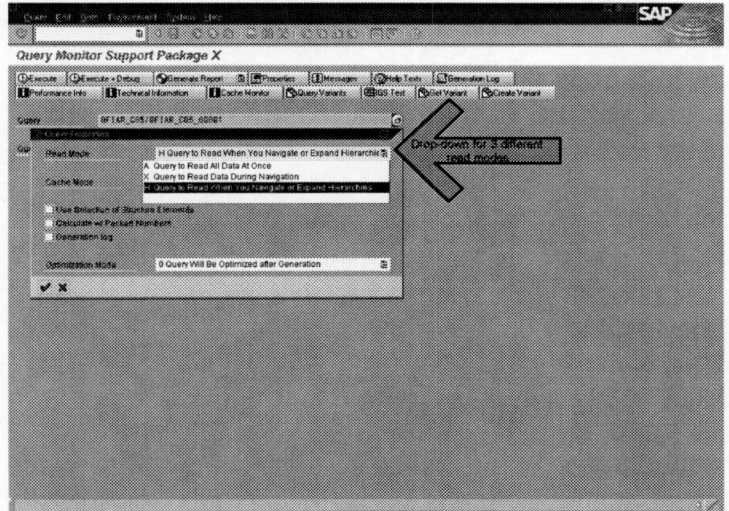

Figure 19: Read modes for a query in transaction RSRT

Question 48: Query Execution

Upon executing a query, you sometimes see certain cells displaying a value '#' instead of actual values. What is the reason for this and what are the remedies?

A: Let us assume that your InfoProvider is an InfoCube. As we know characteristics are in dimension tables and key figures in fact tables. One or more dimensional characteristics may not have a value. This could be because transaction data that you extract from the source system may not have a value for this characteristic (in the source system). Alternatively, your transformation (transfer/update/start routines) rules are not moving any values to this characteristic. This could also be because you have had to add a new characteristic to a dimension after data had been loaded. If you report (without making arrangements for populating this new characteristic) on this cube, obviously this characteristic will have no value every time it's reported on. Sometimes, the problem is not with the characteristic itself but with its attributes, if any. An attribute may not have a value and this is because the corresponding master data does not exist. As an example, if material is a dimensional characteristic and material group is one of its attributes, a new material group (master data) 'ABC' that material 'XYZ' belongs to was not loaded. So, the material group for material 'ABC' is undefined when you report.

The most reliable way to remedy this situation is simple – master data of attributes need to be loaded frequently and in advance of master data for characteristics. Since this is not always feasible, another approach is to filter out the '#' character in the Query Designer. This is a risky approach though as it filters out the entire record that contains the characteristic with the '#' or undefined value. Another technique is to have the 'not assigned' or '#' or any such character/string replaced with blanks or some meaningful description. One way to achieve this is by attaching this logic directly to a query using a VBA (Visual Basic for Access) Macro. This macro is called SAPBEXonRefresh and the replacement can be done using a couple of lines of code.

Question 49: Stylesheets

How do you access and change existing stylesheets and create new ones for use in Web templates?

A: Existing stylesheets are stored in the MIME repository of the Web Application Server. They can be accessed by running transaction SE80 or by taking the following navigation path in your BW system : SAP Menu → Business Explorer → MIME Repository → BW → BCT → Stylesheets.

In order to modify existing stylesheets and to save them as your own you would first have to copy an existing stylesheet in the repository as a template to your local drive. This can be done by highlighting the desired stylesheet and clicking on the right button of the mouse and from the context menu selecting Export and then 'As a Copy'. The next step is to edit this stylesheet in any text editor. Once you are done, you need to save the modified stylesheet in the 'Customer' area of the repository. Carry out the following navigation: SAP Menu → Business Explorer → MIME Repository → BW → Customer → Stylesheets. Highlight the 'Stylesheets' node and right mouse-click and from the context menu select 'Import MIME Objects'. Save the stylesheet with a suitable name.

Question 50: BEx Personalization

What is personalization in BEx and how do you enable it?

A: It enables you to do the following:

1) Lets the user control what is displayed in the History tab/view when you do an 'Open' from the menu bar. This enables convenient selection of the most recently accessed objects such as queries.

2) Variables are filled with user-defined default values. These values are than tied to their respective variables and the user does not have to fill the same value again.

3) In the case of a web application, a user-specific navigational state can be saved for easy future access.

Each of these areas has an ODS where this information is stored. For (1), it is 0PERS_BOD, for (2), it is 0PERS_VER and for (3), it is 0PERS_WTE.

You can run transaction RS_PERS_ACTIVATE or execute the following navigation in the IMG: SAP Netweaver → SAP Business Information Warehouse → Reporting Relevant Settings → General Reporting Settings → Activate Personalization in BEx.

Anurag Barua

Question 51: Restricted Key Figures

What are restricted and calculated key figures?

A: Restricted and calculated key figures are special key figures that are created in the BEx query designer. They are different from 'basic' key figures whose values are created by the OLAP engine and are an original part of an InfoProvider. A restricted key figure is a key figure (basic or restricted or calculated one) with a restriction or filter on one or more characteristics. A calculated key figure on the other hand has nothing to do with characteristic InfoObjects. It a key figure (basic or restricted or calculated one) on which formulas can be applied. The formulas that can be applied fall into 5 categories: basic, boolean, mathematical, trigonometric, data, and percentage. Calculated key figures are useful when the underlying InfoProvider does not provide the required calculation or key figure by itself and thus additional calculations need to be done.

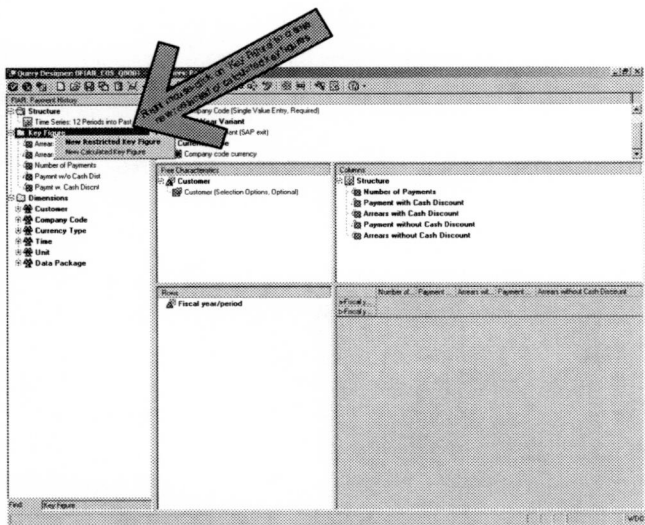

Figure 20: Creating restricted/calculated key figures in the BEx Query Designer

Question 52: Information Broadcasting

What does Information Broadcasting help you achieve and what are the channels via which this information can be disseminated?

A: It is a tool that enables flexible dissemination of information in the BW. This information can be distributed in various formats such as HTML, MHTML, ZIP files, BEx workbooks and from various sources such as BEx queries, workbooks, and web applications such as cockpits and dashboards. It can be made available on demand (i.e. scheduled) on-line or off-line. (To configure and use the Information Broadcasting tool, you need to be on BW release 3.5.)

The two channels via which this information can be disseminated are e-mail and the Enterprise Portal. In the case of e-mail, the information is packaged in the form of precalculated documents or as online links. When a precalculated document changes (because data is added, changed or deleted), the receiver of the e-mail receives the updated document in his/her inbox. In the case of the Enterprise Portal, the most convenient way of accessing this information is via central entry page. This then shows you the content of the Knowledge Management folder where you have published the content.

Question 53: Exception Reporting

What is exception reporting, where can exceptions be created and what are its features?

A: Exceptions enable the identification of deviations in query results. These 'deviations' are defined by the user by setting thresholds. The system aids in visual identification by assigning colors to individual thresholds (in various shades of red, yellow, and green).

Exceptions are created in the Business Explorer (only) and in the following areas:

1) In the Query Designer (by clicking on the exceptions icon and entering desired information).

2) From the toolbar of the standard Web template.

3) In the ad-hoc Query Designer

4) In the web item 'List of Exceptions'

Exceptions or exception reporting can be completely described by the following 3 features:

1) **Exception Definition** – This consists of setting the various parameters (such as setting of alert levels/thresholds, determining cell restrictions) and assigning a name and description to the exception.

2) **Evaluation of Exceptions Online** – Once a query is executed, exceptions are displayed (provided there are any). This step consists of recognizing these exceptions and analyzing them.

3) **Evaluation of Exceptions Offline** – This feature is closely tied to settings made in the Reporting

Agent for background execution of queries. The results are displayed in the alert monitor and exceptions are dumped into the exception log. Using the Reporting Agent, you can schedule any action the system needs to take upon the occurrence of exceptions (such as the triggering of an e-mail).

Question 54: Percentage Functions

Explain the various percentage functions available in formulas for key figures in the BEx query designer.

A: There are 5 percentage functions available in the formula editor:

1) **%; Percentage Deviation; Usage: A%B, where A and B are operands**. This is also known as % deviation and is deviation of A and B; it's a percentage measure of the deviation of A as a % of B.

2) **%A; Percentage Share; Usage: A %A B where A and B are operands.** This is the actual % of A to B.

3) **%CT; Percentage Share of Result; Usage: %CT A where A is an operand.** This shows the values of the key figure A as a % share of the result. The result is the aggregation of the 2nd highest results level.

4) **%GT; Percentage Share of Overall Result; Usage: %GT A where A is an operand.** This shows the values of the key figure A as a % share of the overall result. The overall result is the aggregation of the highest results level and takes dynamic filters into account.

5) **%RT; Percentage Share of Query Result; Usage: %RT A where A is an operand.** This one

is very much like %GT except that dynamic filters are not taken into account when calculating the query result.

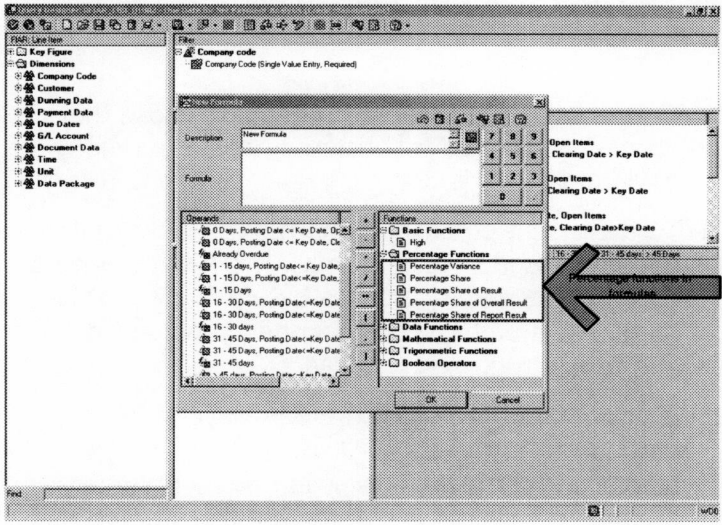

Figure 21: Percentage functions in formulas

Question 55: InfoCube Loading

Describe steps that you should take to optimize loading into and reporting off an InfoCube?

A: Here are the key steps:

1) Define as navigational attributes only those that are absolutely dictated by business needs; too many navigational attributes increase query runtimes

2) To the extent possible, compress the F-table; if uncompressed F-table is small, it is a better idea to drop any secondary indexes before loading. It is takes less time to rebuild secondary indexes then add to existing ones.

3) If your underlying hardware permits, use logical partitioning of the cube. Doing so leads to faster search and retrieval by allowing – among other things – parallel access to the partitions, load balancing etc.

4) If you have a dimension containing a high-cardinality characteristic such as document number, this dimension should not only contain this one characterisitic but it should also be flagged as 'line item' dimension. By doing so, the SID values of these characterisitics are used instead of DIM Ids and thus one table less to join.

5) You should try to reduce the creation and usage of time-dependent charcteristics. Such characteristics require doing a join with the start and end date (i.e. validity period) at run-time. This could be potentially very time-taking.

6) Grouping too many characteristics into one dimension - especially if they are unrelated – often leads to 'dimension explosion' and poor performance. It is better to use smaller logically related dimensions

7) Try to achieve buffering of the number range object for Dim Ids. By doing so, you reserve a block of numbers in memory and prevent the need for accessing the application server each time a new Dim ID is created.

Part V: Performance & Miscellaneous

Question 56: Aggregates

What are aggregates and why are they used?

A: Aggregates are cubes built on cubes and can be considered 'mini-cubes' that generally help optimize query performance. As such, they store subsets of data of an InfoCube in separate tables which have the same structure as the InfoCube. Data in an aggregate can be grouped by different aggregation levels. Each characteristic or navigational attribute of an aggregate must be assigned an aggregation level. This determines the magnitude of compression of the data.

When a query is run on an InfoCube that has an aggregate, it is the aggregate (or the aggregated cube) that is hit and not the InfoCube. You are thus dealing with a reduced subset of the data.

Aggregates are a mixed blessing though. They occupy a lot of space. If you have numerous aggregates, the time taken for an attribute change run following the loading of master data can take up a long time.

Question 57: Aggregate Performance

What are the things you need to check with regards to a query to ensure that building aggregates will enhance performance?

A: An aggregate is likely to improve performance if one or more of the conditions below are true:

1) If the time spent on the database is over 30% of the total runtime of the query that is being investigated. This information can be obtained from table RSDDSTAT and the parameter that contains this information is QDBTIME.

2) If the ratio of records transferred from the database to the records selected is greater than 10%. This information is available in table RSDDSTAT and the parameters that contain this information are QDBTRANS and QDBSEL. A ratio of the 1st parameter to the 2nd will yield the relevant information.

3) Generally speaking, any query that selects roughly over 10,000 records from an InfoCube indicates that the latter might need an aggregate built on it.

4) If the time spent on the database is high for any query, it may mean that aggregation is likely to help. There is no exact benchmark for 'high' but an SAP recommended 3 seconds would be a good rule of thumb.

It is important to note that all these values are recommendations. Aggregates should be built if the designer believes that they are likely to allevate performance bottlenecks even when they compared to lower thresholds.

Question 58: OLAP Cache

What is the OLAP cache ? Why and how do you use it?

A: It is a technique that improves query performance by caching or storing data centrally (main memory or persistent cluster) and thereby making it accessible to various application servers. When the query is run for the first time, the results are saved to the cache so that the next time when a similar query is run, it does not have to read from the data target/database but from the cache. The benefit of this approach is obvious if you consider the fact that the same complex query may be run by various users. Without the OLAP cache, data will have to be fetched from the InfoProvider each time thereby causing inefficient usage of system resources.

Prior to BW Release 3.0B (i.e. starting relase 2.0B and prior to 3.0B), there was no concept of a global OLAP cache. Results were cached for each user and there was no need for configuring the cache – if it grew in size, you would have to manually reduce it's size. With the concept of a shared, global OLAP cache, you have to carry out certain configuration steps. You need to run transaction RZ10 to set the buffer. You then run transaction RSCUSTV14 or (if you are on a SAP Netweaver release) executing the following navigation steps in the IMG Menu (transaction SPRO): SAP Netweaver → SAP Business Information Warehouse → Report-relevant Settings → General Reporting Settings in Business Explorer → Global Cache Settings. You need to set the relevant parameters here.

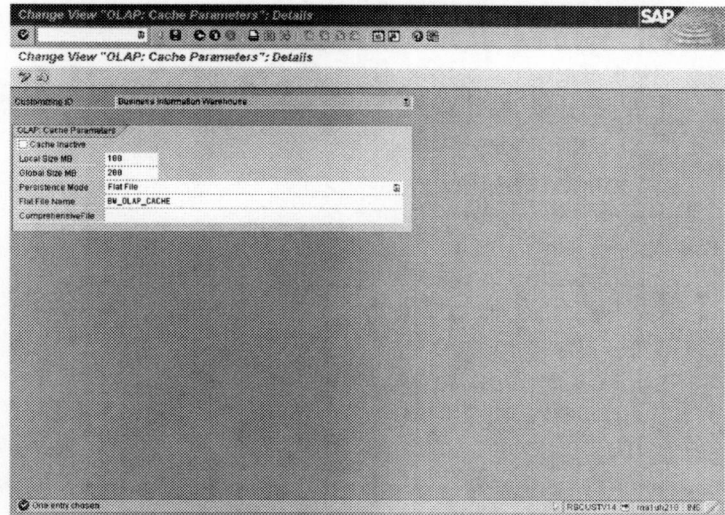

Figure 22: Configuring the global OLAP cache

You can make specific settings for specific InfoProviders (if you feel somewhat constrained by the global settings). These will override the global OLAP cache settings for that specific InfoProvider. You can do so in an SAP Netweaver system by following this navigation: IMG Menu (transaction SPRO): SAP Netweaver → SAP Business Information Warehouse → Report-relevant Settings → General Reporting Settings in Business Explorer → InfoProvider Properties. Enter the InfoProvider name and execute. You can set the cache mode here as shown in **Figure 23:**

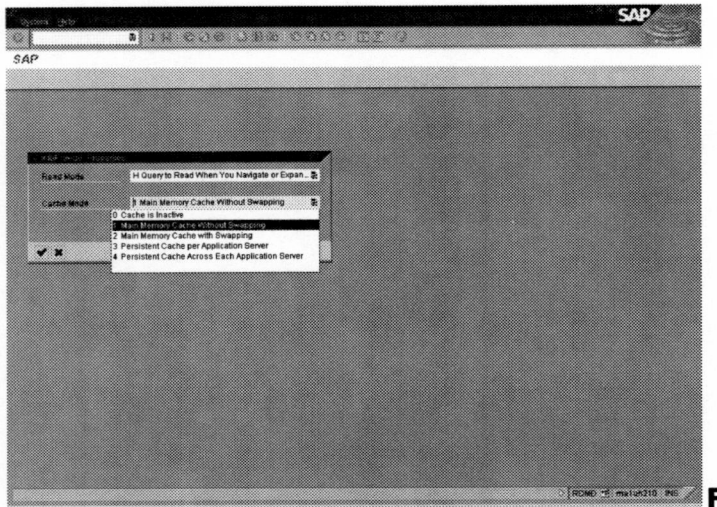

Figure 23: Selecting desired Cache Mode for specific InfoProvider

Finally, you can make settings that override both the global and InfoProvider level settings. These settings will then be applicable to a specific query on a specific InfoProvider. You can do this in transaction RSRT (Query Monitor Support Package). You enter the technical name of the query, click on 'Properties' and a pop-up similar to the one shown in **Figure 23** will be displayed. You will need to select the desired option.

Question 59: Tune Query Performance

What are the major steps you need to take in order to improve and fine-tune query performance?

A: There are several steps you can take. Mentioned below are some of the most important ones:

1) If the intention is not to slice-and-dice but to merely do tabular reporting, reporting should be done on an ODS Object (if one is available) and not on an InfoCube.

2) Complex and large reports should not be run on-line, rather they should be scheduled run durng off-peak hours to avoid excessive contention for limited system resources. You should use the Reporting Agent (RA) to run them during off-peak hours in batch mode.

3) Queries against Remote Cubes should be avoided to the extent possible. This is because a query to a Remote Cube means going across the network and accessing the information that is available in a different system – this causes poor peformance.

4) If you have a choice between using a formula and a calculated key figure, you should opt for the latter. Formulas are computed dynamically during query execution and if they happen to be complicated, the query slows down. On the other hand, calculated

key figures are computed during loading of data to the data target.

5) If you have a choice between using hierarchies and characteristics (or navigational attributes), you should choose characterisitcs or navigational attributes.

6) The tendency to use (i.e. drag-and-drop) characteristics in rows and columns must be avoided. Using characteristics in rows and columns causes the OLAP engine to return a potentially larger volume of data then is actually needed. Moreover, a suitable aggregate may be difficult to find. Instead, if you need to navigate on a certain characteristic, you should place it in the 'free characteristics' area, so that you can drill-down later on.

7) While exceptions and conditions aid in advanced analysis, they should be used as sparingly as possible. They cause an additional overhead on the database and application servers and slow down the query.

8) Whenever feasible, you should use filters.

9) Instead of running the same query each time you need to see the results, you should save the results from the first run in a workbook. Each time you need to run the query, refresh the data. This prevents same data from being repeatedly fetched from the database.

10) Try to keep the size of the query result set as small as possible. You should strive to use the BW system for analytical reporting and not create queries that fetch you all the operational data. Operational reporting is best left to the OLTP system.

Question 60: Partitioning BW

What are the different ways in which partitioning is achieved in a BW system?

A: There are two types of partitioning in BW:

1) **Logical/High-level** – This is achieved by creating multiproviders. They are a logical union of 2 or more InfoProviders. Therefore, they do not consume any additonal database space. They (generally) spawn parallel sub-queries on the constituent InfoProviders. When the sub-query hits a constituent InfoProvider, a reduced set of data is loaded into a smaller InfoCube as opposed to a large set of data into a larget InfoCube in the absence of a multiprovider.

2) **Table/Low-level** – This is physical partioning and can take place only if the underlying database allows it (like Oracle, Informix, IBM DB2/390). One of the common ways to realize this type of partioning is to create ranges. Fact tables of an InfoCube can be partioned based on a time slice like fiscal year, calendar month etc. (You can set up partitioning in InfoCube maintenance. You need to click on 'Extras' from the menu and then select 'Partitioning'. You will get a pop-up as shown in **Figure 24**). Table partitioning cannot be an after-thought, it has to be effected before data are loaded. The benefits of using table partitioning are manifold – significant degree of parallelism can be achieved and leads to better resource utilization. Old data can be quickly removed by dropping a

partition as opposed to actually deleting the data because the former is quicker.

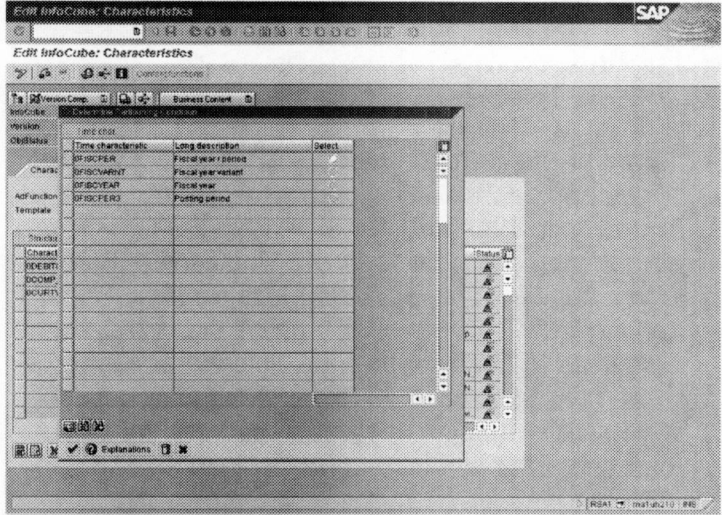

Figure 24: Range Partitioning in an InfoCube

Question 61: Optimization

How can you improve on high extraction times and optimize extractor performance?

A: Some of the common measures you can take are:
1) If you have enhanced an extractor, check your code in user exit RSAP0001 for expensive SQL. statements, nested selects etc. and rectify them
2) If you have several extraction jobs running concurrently, there probably aren't enough system resources to dedicate to any single extraction job – make sure you schedule these jobs judiciously.
3) If you have multiple application servers, try to do load balancing by distributing the load among different servers.
4) Try to increase the number of parallel processes so that packages are extracted parallelly instead of sequentially.
5) Manipulate the size of data packages – the size impacts the way data is extracted from the database tables. The rule of thumb is that in resource-rich systems, you should configure larger package sizes and for resource-constrained systems, smaller package sizes would make more sense. You can carry out the settings outlined in steps (3), (4) and (5) by making the required changes in table ROIDOCPRMS or by running transaction SBIW and then carrying out the following navigation: General Settings → Maintain Control Parameters for Data Transfer.

6) Build secondary indexes on the underlying tables of a DataSource to correspond to the fields in the selection criteria of the DataSource.

7) If your source is not an SAP system but a flat file, make sure that this file is housed on the application server and not on the client machine. Files stored in an ASCII format are faster to load than those stored in a CSV format. If your data file resides on a tape, load it to a disk before extracting. Loading from a disk works invariably faster than loading from tape.

Question 62: PSA Performance

What steps should be taken to improve performance and optimize design on a PSA?

A: The following are the techniques:

1) The PSA needs to be partitioned in order to improve data load performance. Parallel insertions are made possible when the PSA is partitioned because instead of inserting sequentially into one area in memory, it enables you to enter multiple records in parallel into smaller chunks of memory. This can be configured in transaction RSCUTV6 where you can set the package size and the partition size (1 million records is the SAP-provided default). Depending on the size of your data loads you can fine tune this parameter.

2) If you have no need for some old PSA data/tables, they should either be deleted or archived. A well-managed PSA ensures better data load performance.

Question 63: Performance Analysis

Name and briefly describe the most commonly used performance monitoring and analysis tools in BW.

A: BW offers a wide variety of tools for performance monitoring and analysis. Here are the most widely used ones:

1) **Workload analysis** - You use transaction ST03

2) **BW Technical Content analysis** – There is standard Business Content (InfoArea: 0BWTCT) that needs to be activated. It contains several InfoCubes, ODS Objects and multiproviders and contains a variety of performance-related information.

3) **BW Monitor** – You can get to it independently of an InfoPackage by running transaction RSMO or via an InfoPackage. An important feature of this tool is the ability to retrieve important Idoc information.

4) **System trace** – Transaction ST01 lets you do various levels of system trace such as authorization checks, SQL traces, table/buffer trace etc. It is a general Basis tool but can be leveraged for BW.

5) **Performance Analysis** – Transaction ST05 enables you to do performance traces in different areas namely SQL trace, Enqueue trace, RFC trace, and buffer trace.

6) **Database Performance Analysis** – Transaction ST04 gives you all that you need to know about what's happening at the database level.

7) **ABAP runtime analysis tool** – Use transaction SE30 to do a runtime analysis of a transaction, program or function module. It is a very helpful tool if you know the program or routine that you suspect is causing a performance bottleneck.

Question 64: Process Chain Monitoring

What are the various ways by which you can monitor process chains?

A: There are four ways by which you can do so:

1) By using CCMS monitor sets in transaction RZ20. Here, you open the node 'SAP BW Monitors', double-click on 'BW Monitor' and then expand the node for the server you are interested in and then expand the Process Chains node. Alternatively, you can run transaction BWCCMS.

2) You can use transaction SLG1 (Analyze application log).

3) By creating a metachain containing all the process chains you are interested in, you can simulate your own simple dashboard that will show you the status of your chains in different colors.

4) If you are interested in some 3rd party tool, you will have to integrate it with your BW system but you can certainly use such a tool for some value-added monitoring.

Anurag Barua

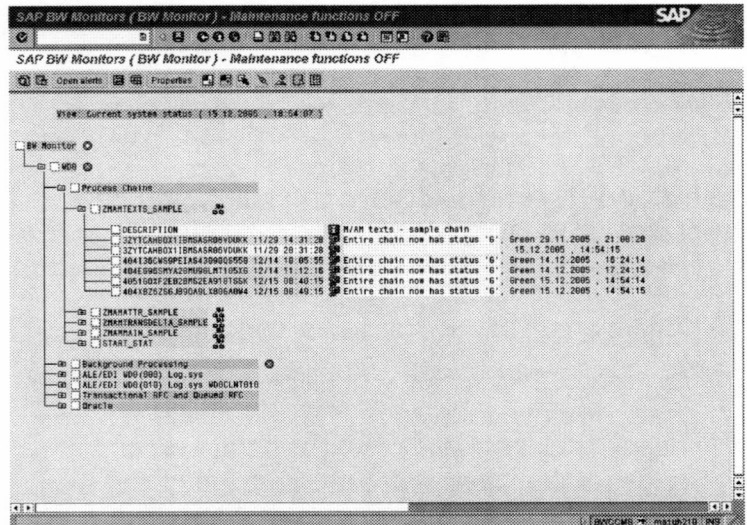

Figure 25: Monitoring of BW process chains in transaction BWCCMS

- 128 -

Question 65: Global Settings

Your BW system is connected to an R/3 source system. What global settings should you transfer from the R/3 source system and how do you do this?

A: There are 5 global settings that can be transferred from R/3 to BW:

1) Currencies

2) Units of Measurement

3) Fiscal Year variants

4) Factory Calendar

5) Exchange Rates

The transfer can be effected from the BW system by carrying out the following navigation as shown below. Click on the modeling tab after executing transaction RSA1; double-click on the 'Source systems' tab; open up the context menu of the R/3 source system you are connected to with a right mouse-click. In the context menu, the last 2 options are 'Transfer Exchange Rates' and 'Transfer Global Settings'. Clicking on the latter option takes care of global settings 1 through 4 in the list above. It takes you to the selection screen of an ABAP report called RSIMPCUST. You will have the option to select one or more of the 4 global settings and also the option to simulate or update or rebuild the corresponding master tables. You want to click on the former if you want to import exchange rates. Once you do so, an ABAP report caleed RSIMPCURR is called. In the selection screen of this report you can specify the exchange rate type and a validity date. You also get the option to simulate or update or rebuild the corresponding master table.

You can consider the first 4 global settings relatively static. This means that you do not have to transfer these settings on a regular basis. Exchange rates are more volatile in nature and you might want to run report RSIMPCURR on a more frequent basis.

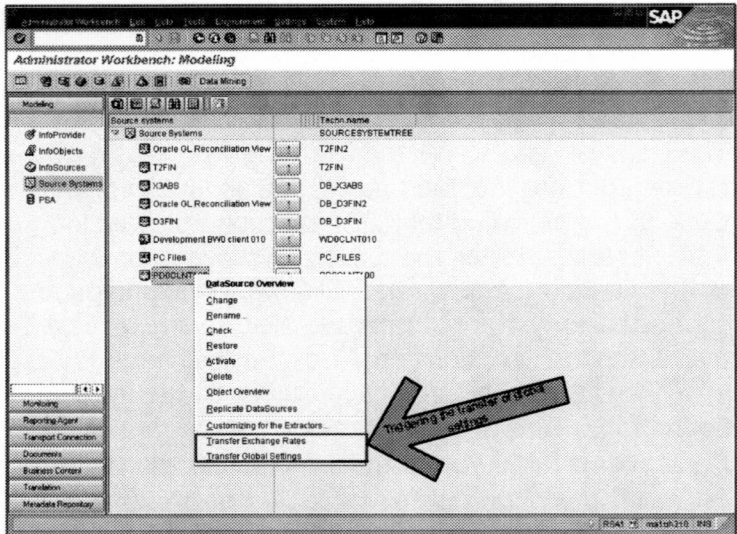

Figure 26: Transfer of global settings from source system tab of Administrator Workbench

Question 66: PSA Data

You are trying browse data in the PSA of an InfoSource. You see some of the requests/data loads but not all. What is the reason for this and how can this problem be rectified?

A: Unless you have deleted one or more of these data loads, the reason that you are not being able to see all the requests is because of a screen setting for the PSA data selection in the PSA tree. It has probably been set to display requests for a short period of time like last week or last month. This situation is easily rectifiable and you do so by clicking on settings (assuming you are already on the PSA screen) and clicking on 'Display Selection for PSA Tree'. It will open up a pop-up window as shown below:

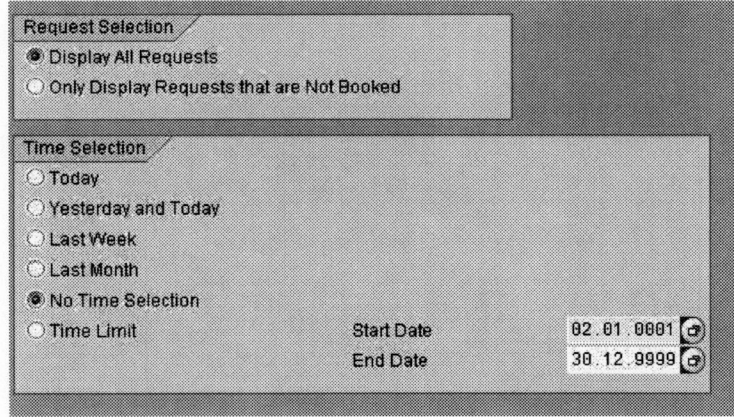

Figure 27: Selection options for displaying PSA tree

The Request Selection section has 2 options:

Display All Requests – All requests (within the time slice you have chosen) - regardless of whether they have been loaded into subsequent data targets or not – are displayed.

Only Display Requests that are not Booked – Choosing this option means only those requests (within the time slice you have chosen) that have been loaded into subsequent data targets are displayed.

Question 67: Report-to-Report Interface

Describe the Report-to-Report Interface (RRI) in BW, its purpose and how to set it up.

A: RRI enables users to jump from one set of information to antoher. This could be from a BEx query to another BEx query or BW Web Application or BW Crystal Report or InfoSet query or transaction or ABAP report or website/URL. The source is called the sender and the target is called the receiver. The link between the sender and receiver (maintained in transaction RSBBS) is possible because meta data in the sender (in BW) is matched up with the meta data in the receiver. The output of the sender is thus populated into the input parameters of the receiver.

The RRI is most commonly used for calling ABAP reports and R/3 transactions (which could themselves trigger reports). To achieve this, the data target on which the query is based ought to have been loaded with data via an InfoSource. In the simplest of cases, this ensures that when you jump back from the data target to R/3, you can use a reverse mapping process that passes the output parameters from the data target to the input parameters of the transaction or the ABAP report. For complex transformations, the reversal can be only done by using customer exits. SAP has provided two: one for meta data transformation (EXIT_SAPLRSBBS_001) and the other for the actual data transformation (EXIT_SAPLRSBBS_002).

You can use the RRI and set up sender-receiver relationships by running transaction RSBBS (as shown in Figure 28):

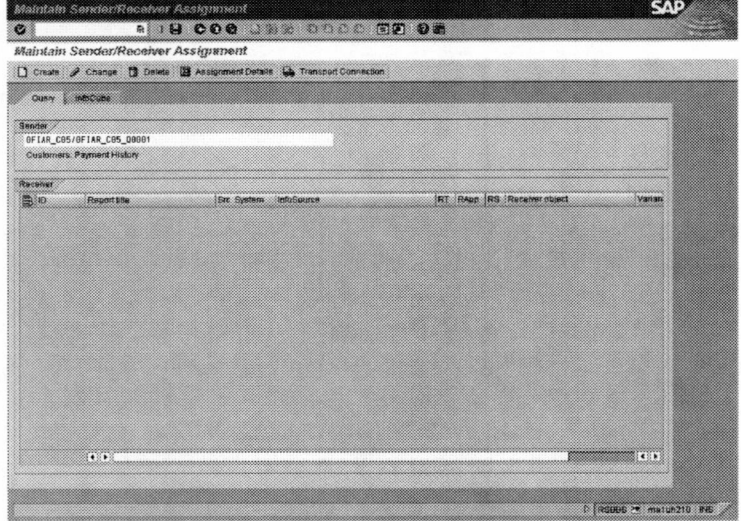

Figure 28: Sender/Receiver Maintenance in RRI

Question 68: RSA1 Grouping

In the transport connection interface of the Administrator Workbench (in transaction RSA1), you can select from 5 different options under the 'Grouping' tab. What are these modes and what does each of them help you in doing?

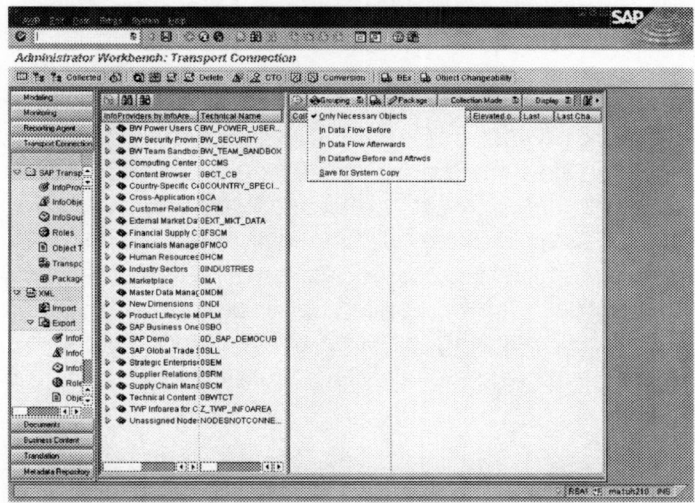

Figure 29: Grouping of BW objects in transports

A: The grouping function/tab helps you identify all the objects that should go together (in a transport) for a given area. This is done automatically by the system when you select an option. There are 5 options that are available for selection:

1) **Only necessary objects** – This is the default and it ensures that whatever objects you have selected (by dragging from the left-hand panel of objects

and dropping on the right hand panel of collected objects) will be considered for transporting.

2) **In dataflow before** – All objects that send data to the collected object are taken into account (and transferred to the right-hand panel of collected objects).

3) **In dataflow after** – All objects that receive data from the collected object are taken into account.

4) **In dataflow before and after** – Choosing this option has the combined effect of choosing options (2) and (3) separately. All objects that send data to and receive data from the collected object are taken into account.

5) **Save for System Copy** – This mode is to be selected only for the purposes of a system copy. It ensures that all objects that are dependent on the source system (such as data sources) are collected in a change/transport request. After a system copy, this request can be applied (or imported) so that the saved mapping between these objects and the source system is not deleted.

Question 69: Multiprovider Parallel Sub-queries

You expect queries on multiproviders to be split into several parallel sub-queries. Is this always the case and if not, how does the OLAP processor determine how many parallel sub-queries to spawn?

A: This is not always the case because the OLAP processor is constrained by the availability of system resources or free dialog work processes to be precise. Upon execution of a query (on a multiprovider), the number of parallel sub-queries is set to two less than the number of available dialog work processes. This can mean that the number of dialog work processes is less than the number of parallel sub-queries. This could result in limited parallelism. Let's assume that your multiprovider is built on top of five InfoCubes. This means that five parallel sub-queries are spawned upon execution of the query. Let's assume that only five dialog work processes are available at run time. This effectively reduces the number of available work processes to three. So, only three parallel sub-queries are shot and once any one of them returns result to a particular synchronization point, this freed-up work process is assigned to the 4th InfoCube and the next freed-up process assigned to the 5th. So, the process becomes less parallel and more pipelined after a certain point and this results in degradation of performance. As might be obvious, a smaller set of base InfoProviders could lead to better parallelism.

ABOUT THE AUTHOR

Anurag Barua has over 13 years of experience in conceiving, designing, managing and implementing complex software solutions including 8 years of SAP experience. He has been associated with several SAP implementations in various capacities. He worked at SAP Labs for 5 years. Anurag's core SAP competencies extend beyond BW/BI and include FI/CO, Logistics, Netweaver, ABAP, SOX compliance, reporting, and project management. He has a B.S. in Computer Science from India and an MBA in Finance from the University of Maryland at College Park. Anurag lives in Germantown, Maryland with his wife and two children.

CPSIA information can be obtained at www.ICGtesting.com
Printed in the USA
BVOW040831300512

291360BV00001B/331/A